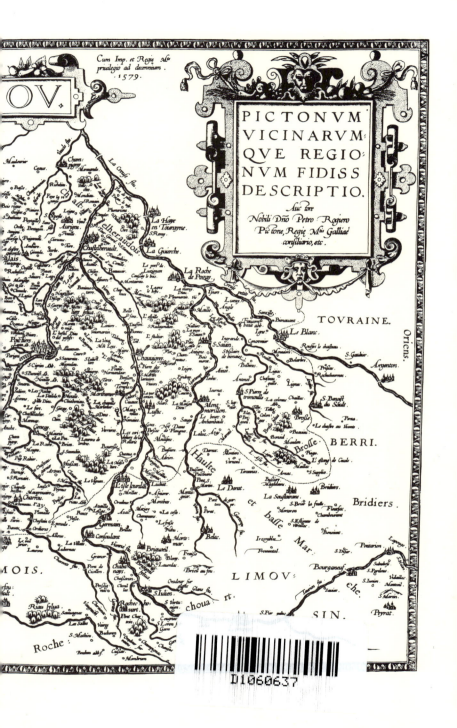

HIS LIFE, TO HIS CHILDREN

Theodore-Agrippa
d'Aubigné

HIS·LIFE,
to
His Children

Sa Vie à ses enfants

TRANSLATED,

WITH AN INTRODUCTION

AND NOTES,

BY JOHN NOTHNAGLE

University of Nebraska Press

Lincoln & London

Copyright © 1989 by the University of Nebraska Press
All rights reserved
Manufactured in the United States of America

The paper in this book meets the minimum requirements
of American National Standard for
Information Sciences – Permanence of Paper for Printed
Library Materials, ANSI Z39.48-1984

Library of Congress Cataloging in Publication Data
Aubigné, Agrippa d', 1551-1630.
[Sa vie à ses enfants. English]
His life, to his children = Sa vie à ses enfants /
by Theodore-Agrippa d'Aubigné; translated,
with an introduction and notes, by John Nothnagle.
p.   cm.
Translation of: Sa vie à ses enfants.
Bibliography: p.
Includes index.
ISBN 0-8032-1682-3 (alk. paper)
1. Aubigné, Agrippa d', 1551-1630 – Biography.
2. Poets. French –16th century – Biography.
3. Huguenots – France – Biography.
I. Title.
PQ1603.A82613   1989
841'.3 – dc19   [B]   88-20491   CIP

Endleaf map: The province of Poitou,
d'Aubigné's home country.
From Abraham Ortelius's *Theatrum
orbis terrarum,* London, 1606

Contents

Translator's Introduction   vii

Preface   3

I   Childhood and Youth, 1552–1570   5

II   A Mistress and a Master, 1570–1576   18

III   Into Action and Out of Favor, 1576–1579   32

IV   Marriage amid War and Intrigue, 1579–1583   44

V   Campaigning for a Kingdom, 1583–1589   56

VI   Bitter Victory, 1590–1610   74

VII   Early Retirement, 1610–1620   90

VIII   "No Separate Peace," 1620–1630   102

Appendix A: The Rival Clans   121

Appendix B: A Religious Conversion?   125

Notes   129

Index   175

bon celuy-là pour la plume
et pour le poil, car il est bon
capitaine et soldat, très sçavant, et
très éloquent et bien disant,
s'il en fut onc.

BRANTÔME
Discours sur les Courennels
de l'Infanterie
de la France

Translator's Introduction

Théodore-Agrippa d'Aubigné lived from 1552 to 1630, a man of many parts, as Brantôme knew, in an age that had use for them all. His place in the French chapter of the history of that time is small but impressive, for he was a witness to, and often participated in, many of its great events. He fought for the Huguenot cause in the wars of religion, where he proved himself an intransigent partisan and a master of the art of small or guerrilla war. He observed the decline and extinction of the Valois dynasty, attended the first Bourbon king, Henry of Navarre, in his campaigns for the throne of France, and resisted the drive toward absolutism that brought Richelieu to power.

More important in the perspective of time, he was a man of letters, a writer whose energy and talent were lavished on a body of work of remarkable variety. He wrote in French and in Latin, in prose and in poetry, the latter in traditional and innovative French forms and in experimental measured verse. His works include *Le Printemps*, a collection of lyric poetry in three books, largely inspired by an unhappy love affair of his youth; *Les Tragiques* in seven books, an intense and moving poetic response to the wars of religion and to the agony and glory of the Huguenot cause; the boisterous and amusing *Avantures du baron de Faeneste*; the bitterly satirical *Confession catholique du sieur de Sancy*. In addition there are isolated poems, religious and political tracts and commentaries, and an extensive correspondence covering subjects as varied as the education of women, military science, witchcraft and the occult, and his personal and financial concerns.

In his later years he wrote a comprehensive history of his time, covering the years from 1553, when Henry of Navarre was born, to 1602. He called it grandly his *Histoire universelle*. As history the work is flawed by d'Aubigné's understandable conviction of the righteousness of the Huguenot cause and by his belief that "from this narrative you will draw the meaning of all true history, which is to know, through the folly and weakness of man, the judgment and the face of God" (1:10). In detail, however, the *Histoire* is rich in vigorous and exciting accounts of action, noble gestures, resounding calls to conscience or to arms. It deserves to be better known.

As a companion piece to the *Histoire universelle* he wrote a story of his life that he reserved for his children. He entitled it accordingly *Sa Vie à ses enfants*. The frequent references that he makes in it to the *Histoire universelle* indicate that he must have written it after he had completed the publication of the latter in 1620, thus when he was living in exile in Geneva. This dating would agree with the implication in the preface that his surviving children were not only grown but living apart from him. However, one of the daughters to whom he addressed it died in 1625, and there is a reference at the end of the text to the fall of La Rochelle, which occurred in 1628. It seems likely, then, that he wrote *Sa Vie* intermittently throughout the whole decade of the 1620s in

Geneva, at the same time that he resumed the composition of his *Histoire* to bring it up to date.

D'Aubigné intended that *Sa Vie* be the private and personal account of his life, separate from but complementary to the formal, professedly objective, history from which he had largely effaced himself. Such concern for the self—to hide it in the public record, to assert it in the private—bespeaks an egotism that is remarkable in its magnitude and in its delicacy. So we should not be unduly surprised to find the book written in the third person, a narrative device worthy perhaps of Caesar, Richelieu, even De Gaulle, but unexpected from the pen of a man writing to his children. The third-person narration has, of course, the advantage of minimizing confusion or ambiguity between the author and his subject, between the "I" who writes and the remembered "me" that is written about, but the extent to which an autobiographer benefits from this distancing remains uncertain. It may perhaps foster the scrupulous objectivity expected of the serious historian. But it might also lead the author, now a spectator of himself, into the temptation of voyeurism if he finds unseemly pleasure in the recording and arranging of the details of his life, especially when a flattering or consoling pattern can be discerned. In either case, the main problem of biography, or autobiography, remains, and a life is cast in the role of a literary character. With d'Aubigné the role is that of the hero, and the influence of heroic biography in its elaboration is evident. The tragic circumstances of his birth, his banishment from the father's house, his intellectual precocity, the early marks of a special destiny, reflect the conventions of a genre which requires a child-hero to announce or prefigure future exploits. It might be noted in this regard that d'Aubigné opened his *Histoire* with a chapter describing the birth and Spartan childhood of another hero, Henry of Navarre—who then promptly disappears from the narrative until he is of an age to play a public role. D'Aubigné's life reads like an unbroken series of adventures, achievements, artful conversations, or debates that create the character that the author thought himself to be. Even his rare defeats and embarrassments hint of glory. Only at the end of *Sa Vie*, in d'Aubigné's account of the misdeeds of his son, Constant, does the heroic mask fall and a perception emerge of the real man in his pain and frustration.

There should then be neither surprise nor distress that *Sa Vie* may distort the reality that it purports to tell. If d'Aubigné had attempted with greater determination to convey the raw truth of his life he would still have failed, and in this failure distorted its truth even more. Besides, what we possess is in fact a worthy reality: a well-told life story, coherent, highlighted with bold actions and stirring words, flashes of wit, recurring drama, and a confirmation of the passionate and chaotic spirit of the late Renaissance.

For these reasons, and to make known an extraordinary writer heretofore available only to specialists in the literature or history of his period, I have put his story into English, compounding thereby the violation of privacy that he enjoined upon his children. As I worked with the text I learned early on that translation can be as difficult a challenge as biography or autobiography, not so much for the obscure historical references and the archaic vocabulary that occur in the present case, but for the style of its prose. It is said in French that style is the man, and d'Aubigné supports the point. His prose is that of action, exploding through a stream of participial constructions to create a sense of multifaceted and simultaneous movements, in the manner of cinema rather than of prose narration. But it remains prose narration, and style since d'Aubigné's time has become analytical, insisting that correct temporal and causal relations be observed. For the sake of clarity, therefore, I had to slow his swirling and often tumultuous movement with subordinate clauses, recall vanishing antecedents, and tag his vigorous verbal thrusts with what I felt to be indispensable conjunctions. To be honest with original texts I have set such additions between brackets and attentive readers can judge for themselves the merits of the change.

*

Since d'Aubigné wrote *Sa Vie* for his children and could rely on their familiarity with his world as well as with the *Histoire*, he provided no explanations or background information. For the modern reader, therefore, extensive annotation is in order as well as a cursory sketch of the historical situation in which d'Aubigné lived. I hope you will read these addenda, for they constitute an essential dimension of *Sa Vie*.

In the latter part of the sixteenth century, France was physically smaller than it is today, and its land borders formed a ragged and perilous edge. The river Somme marked the northern frontier, beyond which lay the Netherlands, a Spanish possession by dynastic accident. To the east the Meuse and the Saône separated France from imperial territories, although vestiges of earlier feudal settlements left enclaves on either side of the border. The Franche-Comté belonged to Philip II of Spain by inheritance. To the south the frontier was approximately drawn by the Rhone, to the east of which lay imperial, papal, and Savoyard possessions. The wall of the Pyrenees was broken to the west by what remained of the kingdom of Navarre and to the east by Roussillon, a dependency of Catalonia, and thus of Spain. France was, therefore, closely ringed by lands governed either by Spain, then at the height of her power, or by the empire, dynastically and ideologically linked to Spain, or by the Duchy of Savoy, an occasional Spanish ally. Within these borders there lived a population of some fifteen million to sixteen million people. Except for Paris there was no really large city, and regional differences were sharply marked by the vigorous survival of feudal arrangements and local custom and privilege.

In this restless mosaic of premodern France, the southwest, where d'Aubigné spent much of his life—Poitou, Vendée, Aunis, and Saintonge—merits special attention. Its coastline was different from what it is today because the extensive reclamation work which has pushed the sea many miles to the west and made of the tidal flats dry and productive land had only recently been started. In d'Aubigné's time it was still a low and marshy place, studded with patches of high ground known as islands, and plagued with malarial tertian and quartan agues. The economy on the whole was agricultural, favored by the availability of river transportation. Trade and commerce, the main generators of wealth in the Renaissance, were not practiced except in the port towns. Of these La Rochelle was the most prosperous and the most aggressive in the defense of its privileges and monopolies. In contrast, the interior seemed a poor region. However, the relentless inflation that drove up the prices of agricultural products in the second half of the sixteenth century led to an appreciation in land values. The owners, the gentry of Poitou and Vendée, knew the value of their land. But they were also aware that it was incapable of producing quick wealth in negotiable form as did the commerce of the merchants of La Rochelle or the charges and endowments conferred upon court favorites and ecclesiastical appointees. Their relative poverty amid such wealth may explain their conservative ways, their susceptibility to the attractions of

Protestantism, and their readiness to take up arms to defend their estates or to seize new ones.

France as a whole remained a monarchy obedient to its ancient unwritten constitution, but to an observer who viewed the situation at practically any point between the death of Henry II in 1559 and the coronation of Henry IV in 1594, the future of the nation looked uncertain at best. There was reason for such pessimism. France had exhausted herself during the first half of the century in a costly and fruitless struggle with Spain. In addition, the absolutist policies of the powerful Francis I had created great internal pressures and a frustrated and impoverished nobility. How Francis's successor, Henry II, might have handled this explosive situation remains unknown, since he was fatally injured in a joust. And for the added misfortune of the kingdom, his three sons who succeeded to the throne, Francis II, Charles IX, and Henry III, were inept, morally weak, and physically ravaged. To compensate for their weakness the queen mother, Catherine de Médicis, came to play an increasingly important role in the governance of the kingdom. The main policy she pursued in the face of her multiple adversities was a basic one: to preserve the monarchy as the patrimony of her family. And her means were those of desperation: compromise, accommodation, expediency. Still, she might have succeeded if her last son had had an heir. But when Henry III proved childless her policy and her will collapsed, and anarchy followed.

The problems that Catherine and her sons faced were overwhelming. As if responding to a signal from history, the monarchy wished itself absolute, to fashion for itself a politically and economically centralized state, for to such states the future would belong. But the past, in the persons and ambitions of the great noble houses—Lorraine, Montmorency, Bourbon—and of the lesser nobles who by habit and ambition were quick to rally to them, resisted such change. Given the weakness of the monarchy the great families might well have triumphed had they been able to settle the differences that divided them. (A description of these families and of their rivalries is given in appendix A).

The political conflicts were further aggravated by a religious one. Since the 1520s the Protestant Reformation had won a growing number of followers in France. At first they seemed prayerfully resigned to remain an oppressed minority. But by the 1550s certain members of the great families (notably Antoine de Bourbon, Gaspard de Coligny, and the first prince of Condé) had embraced the new religion and thereby discovered that the growing Protestant minority, by now known as the Huguenots, might provide the popular support and the ideological fervor to transform feudal resistance to royal ambition into a conservative revolution. When these first princely leaders were killed off in the subsequent warfare, the party they had formed was taken over by its religious leadership and given a popular base with the cover of legitimacy that a prince of the royal blood, Condé's son or Navarre, could provide. Thus strengthened, it could demand not only religious toleration but equal status with Catholicism, recognition of its internal organization, representation in courts and on juries, equal access to titles and charges, and the right to maintain strongholds from which these rights and privileges could be enforced. These were the kinds of demands to which Catherine would yield when circumstances dictated. But their concession infuriated the Catholics who, spurred by a resurgent papacy and the zeal of the Counter-Reformation, formed an opposing party, the Holy League. The House of Lorraine captured the leadership of the League and used it as its own weapon against the king. Thus, in the last years of his reign Henry III had to contend with two states within his state, each with its leadership, its agenda, and its army.

The disorders created by these conflicts were exacerbated by the foreign connections. The warring factions did not hesitate to seek support from sympathetic powers, and these, from a tangle of motives, welcomed the opportunity to intervene in French affairs. German Protestants were the first to come, in the form of the *reîtres*, mercenary cavalrymen dressed, as d'Aubigné wrote in *Les Tragiques*, "in black and in fury." While they were sustained by a spirit of ideological solidarity and content with the prospect of booty, the Protestant princes who sponsored them could entertain the hope that success in France might help them capture a vote or two in the imperial electoral college and thus wrest the empire away from the Catholic House of Habsburg. This was something that Philip of Spain, a fellow Habsburg and self-appointed leader of Catholic Europe, was determined to prevent. But he was bedeviled by more immediate challenges, the most grievous being the revolt in the Netherlands sparked by the Calvinists of the northern provinces, who easily found common cause with the French Huguenots. And his most dramatic challenge arose from the insolences of England, where Elizabeth had imposed a Protestant settlement. She exploited unrest in France to frustrate Spain in the Netherlands, and Philip in turn sought French support, or at least acquiescence, to get at England. Thus, over a period of many years the powers meddled freely in French internal affairs under the pretense of supporting national movements, while in fact furthering their own ambitions and designs. But for the remarkable military and diplomatic skills of Henry of Navarre, who succeeded to the throne at the end of the century and replaced the hapless

Valois, France might well have suffered the fate of Poland two centuries later, or the one that she herself had narrowly avoided in the shifting currents of the Hundred Years' War a century before.

A NOTE ON TEXTS

Most of d'Aubigné's work, except for the history, was edited and published in the last century by Eugène Réaume and F. de Caussade, *Oeuvres complètes de Théodore-Agrippa d'Aubigné*, 6 vols. (Paris: Alphonse Lemerre, 1873–1892; repr. Geneva: Slatkine, 1967). A miscellany of additional texts, omitted from this first publication, were brought out by Pierre-Paul Plan as *Pages inédites de Théodore-Agrippa d'Aubigné* (Geneva: Société d'Histoire et d'Archéologie, 1945). More available than either of the above is the partial but beautifully done edition in the Bibliothèque de la Pléiade series: *Agrippa d'Aubigné: Oeuvres*, edited by Henri Weber with notes by Henri Weber, Jacques Bailbé and Marguerite Soulié (Paris: Gallimard, 1969).

D'Aubigné designed his *Histoire universelle* in three volumes of five books each, each book in turn composed of chapters. He printed the first volume on his own press at Maillé in 1616, the second in 1618, and the third in 1620. He published a much-improved second edition in 1626, ostensibly in Amsterdam but in fact in Geneva.

The first and until recently only modern edition of the *Histoire universelle* was that of Baron Alphonse de Ruble, published in ten volumes for the Société d'Histoire de France (Paris: Librairie Renouard, 1886–1909). In this edition the books, which were numbered by volume in d'Aubigné's editions, are simply numbered consecutively. Since 1981 the Librairie Droz has been publishing a new and most promising edition of the *Histoire universelle* in its

Textes littéraires français series, edited with introduction and notes by André Thierry, who has followed the example of de Ruble and numbered the books consecutively. Because this project has not been completed, my references will be to the de Ruble edition by volume, book, and page numbers and I have accordingly altered d'Aubigné's own references in the text of *Sa Vie*. Thus far these book and chapter numbers are valid for the new Textes littéraires edition as well. An unfinished continuation of the *Histoire* remained in manuscript until it was published by Jean Plattard as the *Supplément à l'Histoire universelle d'Agrippa d'Aubigné* (Paris: Librairie ancienne Champion, 1925).

Sa Vie à ses enfants has survived in a number of manuscript copies, the best of which is thought to be manuscript 156 of the Tronchin Collection in the Bibliothèque publique et universitaire of Geneva. This copy, which serves as the basis for my translation, has been printed in volume 1 of Réaume and Caussade's *Oeuvres complètes*, in the Pléiade edition (pp. 383–463), and in a critical edition by Gilbert Schrenk (Paris: Société des Textes Français Modernes, 1986).

There is also a single edition of the text that was published by Jean Prévost in 1928 (Paris: Gallimard). It is an undistinguished effort, but I am nevertheless indebted to it for two ideas which I have adopted for the present translation: the division of the text into chapters, to which I have given titles, and the insertion of passages from the *Histoire universelle* when d'Aubigné makes specific reference to them. These selections, as well as the occasional pieces of poetry that occur, are in my translation also.

HIS LIFE, TO HIS CHILDREN

Preface

To Constant, Marie, and Louise d'Aubigné.[1]

My Children,

    With its lives of the emperors and of heroes antiquity has provided you with all that you need to draw lessons and precepts by which you might protect yourselves from the attacks of enemies and of rebellious subjects. From the ancients you can learn how they dealt with the insolence of their rivals and the insurrections of their peoples. But what you will not learn from them is how to bear the burden of oppression that weighs down from above. And with this third kind of trouble demanding more deftness than the other two, you have greater need to follow [the lives of] ordinary rather than of great persons, because in the struggle you have with your peers, you have but your own skill for a shield. This is something that princes have failed to learn, and they let themselves fall of their own weight. Henry the Great did not like his men wasting their time with the lives of the emperors; and finding Neuvy too absorbed in his Tacitus, and fearing lest its heroic spirit get the better of him, he advised him to look into the life story of one of his companions.[2]

    This is what I am doing now in honoring your reasonable

3

request: here is the story of my life, in paternal privacy, so that I need not conceal that which in the *Histoire universelle* would have been in poor taste to tell. Thus, unable to blush before you, either for my name or for my shame, I will tell of the one as of the other as if I still held you on my knee. I wish that my fortunate or noble exploits might without envy inspire your emulation, provided that you heed even more closely the faults that I also lay bare before you as the more useful part of my spoils. Study them, for they are my own; but successes are not ours, they come from above.

I must yet demand that there be only two copies of this book, entrusting them to your care, and that you never let them out of the house. If you fail in this, your disobedience will be punished by the envious, who will hold up for scorn the wonders of God as shown in my deliverances, and who will contemn your foolish vanity.

ONE

*

Childhood and Youth

1552-1570

Théodore-Agrippa d'Aubigné, son of Jean d'Aubigné, Lord of Brie in Saintonge, and of Demoiselle Catherine de l'Estang, was born in the manor house of Saint-Maury near Pons, the eighth day of February in the year 1551,[1] his mother dying in childbirth, and in such desperate circumstances that the physicians had to choose between her death or the child's. He was named Agrippa (as in *aegre partus* [birth with pain]) and raised in the beginning away from the house of his father because Anne de Limur, his new stepmother, resented both the expense and the excellent care that the father lavished on him.[2]

When he was four years old the father brought from Paris to be his tutor Jean Cottin, a harsh man and cruel, who taught him Latin, Greek, and Hebrew all at the same time.[3] This method was followed by his second tutor, Peregim, with the result that at the age of six years he read in four languages. Later there was brought for him Jean Morel, a Parisian of some renown, who treated him more gently.

It was at that age that d'Aubigné, lying awake in bed one night waiting for his tutor, heard enter the room, and then approach his bed, a person whose garments rustled against

5

the curtains, which he saw thereupon drawn apart; and a woman, all in white, gave him a kiss which was as cold as ice; and then she disappeared. When Morel arrived he found the boy unable to speak. And what afterward made his story of such a vision credible was a continued fever that lasted fourteen days.

At the age of seven and a half years he translated, with the help of his lessons, the *Crito* of Plato on the promise of his father to have it published with his picture placed at the front of the book.

When he was eight and a half the father took him to Paris. As they rode through Amboise on a market day the father saw the heads of his Amboise companions, still recognizable on what remained of a gallows, and he was so aroused that in the midst of seven or eight thousand people he cried out: "The murderers, they have beheaded France!"[4] The son, seeing an uncommon passion on the father's face, spurred up to him, whereupon he placed his hand on the boy's head and said to him, "My son, your head must not be spared after I am dead to avenge these leaders so rich in honor. If you spare yourself in this you will have my curse." Such words inflamed the crowd, and even though his party included twenty armed horsemen, it had great difficulty in getting away.

In Paris our schoolboy was placed in the care of Mathieu Béroalde, a nephew of the well-known scholar Vatable.[5] At the same time, or soon after, when the prince of Condé had seized Orleans, the persecutions redoubled.[6] The massacres and burnings taking place in Paris forced Béroalde, after many dangers, to flee from the city with his family. It distressed the little boy greatly to have to leave a library of richly bound books and other handsome furnishings, whose beauty had eased his homesickness. Thus, when they were coming near Villeneuve-Saint-Georges the thought of this loss brought tears to his eyes. Béroalde, taking him by the hand, said to him: "My friend, do you not feel the joy it is for you to be able, at your age, to lose something for Him who gave all to you?"

From there this company of four men, three women, and two children, having procured a coach at Le Coudret (the house of the president de L'Estoile), made their way to the village of Courance. Here they were taken prisoner by the chevalier d'Achon, commanding one hundred light horse, who thereupon turned them over to an inquisitor named Democarès.[7] D'Aubigné cried not from fear of prison but because they took away his little sword, beautifully silver-plated, and his silver-studded belt. The inquisitor interrogated him separately, and not without anger at his answers. The captains, however, taking note of his white satin suit with its weltings of silver embroidery and of mannerisms that caught their fancy, conducted him to Achon's room, where they gave him to understand that his whole group was condemned to burn and that there would be no time to recant at the execution. He answered that his horror of the mass left him with no fear of the stake. Now there were some fiddlers there, and as they were dancing Achon asked his little prisoner to do a *gaillarde*, which he did, winning thereby the admiration and affection of his captors, when the inquisitor returned and, hurling insults at everyone, had him put back behind bars. Through him Béroalde learned that their fate had been decided; he took the pulse of his companions to check their courage and to reconcile them to their death.

That evening, as their food was brought in, there was pointed out to them the executioner from Milly, making ready for the morrow. The door then being locked again, the group began to pray. About two hours later a gentleman from Achon's troop came in; he had been a monk and now was in charge of the prisoners. He kissed d'Aubigné on the cheek, then turned to Béroalde and said, "I will either die or I will save you all for the love of this child. Hold yourselves ready to get out of here when I tell you. Meanwhile, give me fifty or sixty crowns to bribe two men without whom I can do nothing for you." We did not waste any time finding sixty crowns hidden in our shoes. At midnight this gentleman returned with the other two. He said to Béroalde: "You told me that the father of this little man was in command in Orleans. Promise me that I will be well received in his companies." That being assured him as well as a proper reward, he had them take one another by the hand and he, taking the hand of the youngest, then led them quietly by the guards to a barn beyond their coach, then through wheatfields to the main road to Montargis, where, after great effort and fear, they finally arrived.

The duchess of Ferrara received them in Montargis with her customary civility, and especially d'Aubigné, whom she kept by her side seated on a cushion for three days listening to his boyish speeches on contempt for death.[8] Then she had them all properly taken to Gien, where they stayed for a month with the royal procurator, Chazeray. But then La Fayette began his siege of the town. They had to take to boats and flee to Orleans, braving harquebus volleys that the villagers near Bouteille fired at them.

In Orleans, through the good offices of the sieur d'Aubigné, who was in command of the city under Monsieur de Saint-Cyr, Béroalde was properly lodged, at first in the house of the president de L'Estoile. Here d'Aubigné was the first to taste the plague that caused the death of thirty thousand people. He saw his surgeon and four others die in his room, among them Madame Béroalde. His servant, named Eschalart and who has since died a minister in Brittany, never left his side and cared for him the whole time without ever taking sick himself, for he always had a psalm on his lips as a preservative.

The sieur d'Aubigné, after having gone to Guyenne to bring up more troops, found on his return that his son was cured but that he had become unruly, because it is difficult *Pacis artes colere inter Martis incendia* [to cultivate the arts of peace amid the flames of war]. One day he sent his clerk to the boy with a garment of coarse wool and instructions to take him out among the shops to choose a trade, since he had forsaken learning and honor. Our scholar took this harsh rebuke so to heart that he fell into a delirium fever and almost died. When he recovered he went before his father to deliver, on his knees, an oration whose pathos brought tears to the listeners. Their reconciliation was marked by a gift his father could ill afford.

Toward the end of that year with the city under siege and Béroalde lodged in the Queen's House, or Cloître Saint-Agnan, the soldiers were again leading the boy astray, and they even took him out among the earthworks, where he was when Monsieur de Duras was killed.[9] One day his father took him to see the sieur d'Achon, who, like the constable, was now in the custody of the sieur d'Aubigné, who had brought them back prisoners from the battle of Dreux.[10] Achon, held in the new tower in a room where there were two small cannons on the floor, was quite astonished to see his little prisoner, who now rebuked him for his inhumanity, although without abuse. For he replied to those who wished him to do so that he could not *insultare afflicto* [taunt a man who was down].

In those days fourteen captains shook hands on a vow to

try to retake the Tourelles, but there were only six who kept their word and jumped into the trenches. It was there that the sieur d'Aubigné received a pike wound under his cuirass. It was half-healed when he was chosen for the peace negotiations, which he attended by crossing in a boat to the Poule Blanche in Portereau, where the queen was staying.[11] He was the fourth in rank for his party to enter the violet pavilion in the Isle aux Boeufs, where the peace was signed.

Because of his role in this treaty and of his other services he was given the office of Maître des Requêtes, to serve as chancellor for the cause.[12] The Sieur de Cavagnes succeeded him in this office after his death.

Once the peace had been made he said good-bye to his son, commending to him his words at Amboise, zeal for the religion, love of learning, and true friendship. Then, against his custom, he kissed him. He went away to Amboise, weakening from an abscess that formed in his wound. And there he died, regretting nothing of this world but that the age of his son would not allow him to succeed to his estate. He said these things as he clutched the letters that he wanted sent to the prince of Condé, begging that they not be entrusted to a man who was not ready to die for God.

It happened that six or seven days after his death two of his men returned to Orleans to take inventory of the arms and baggage that he had left there. In the entrance to the house they found young d'Aubigné, who on seeing them felt in his heart a premonition of his father's death. He hid so that he could look at their expressions as they stabled their horses, and he was so confirmed in his feelings that for three months he would slip away to cry and, despite the reassurances of others, he wore no other dress than mourning.

He had as a guardian Aubin d'Abeville,[13] who, because

of the enormous debts of the father, made him renounce his paternal inheritance of 4,000 pounds in rents and supported him for his studies with money from his mother's property. He left him [in Orleans] for another year in the care of Béroalde, and then, when he was thirteen years old, sent him to Geneva. By that time he could compose more Latin verses than a diligent pen could copy. He read rabbinical Hebrew fluently without [the help of] vowel signs, and explained one language in the other without recourse to the one that he was explaining. He had done his course in philosophy and some mathematics. Nevertheless, for not knowing some of the dialects in Pindar, they placed him back in a college when he had already studied two years in Orleans. That caused him to hate letters, to look on his studies as a burden, and to resent correction. So he began to learn juggling and tricks of legerdemain, which even won him some applause. Monsieur de Bèze was willing to pardon them as tricks of the hare with nothing of the fox, but his teachers were real Orbilies.[14] So, after two years in Geneva he came to Lyons without telling his relatives and began to study mathematics again.[15] He also dabbled in the study of magic, asserting, however, that he did not wish to try experiments with it.[16] But he had no money in Lyons. When the innkeeper's wife pressed him for payment, he became so upset that he dared not return to his room. He spent a whole day without eating, and his melancholy grew. Perplexed to know where he would spend the night he stopped on the bridge over the Saône and bowed his head to let the tears fall freely into the water below. Suddenly he felt an impulse to throw himself after them. All of his troubles spurred him to do it when he remembered that he had been taught that one must first pray to God before undertaking any action. The last words of the prayer he uttered were "life everlasting," and they frightened him. He called out in his anguish to God for help. Then, looking back along the bridge, he saw a servant whom he recognized first by the red trunk that he was carrying, and next the master, who was his cousin, the sieur de Chillaud, on his way to Germany for Monsieur l'Amiral and carrying money to Geneva for our despondent young man.[17]

Soon after began the second war.[18] D'Aubigné returned to his guardian's house in Saintonge. The latter, seeing his ward straining on the leash in his eagerness to get away from his books and join the armies, prudently kept him a prisoner until the third war broke out.[19]

His friends had promised him that they would fire a harquebus when they left for the war. [On hearing the shot] our prisoner, whose clothing was regularly taken from him each evening and kept on a table in his guardian's room, slipped out the window and down the wall of the house with the help of his bed linen. In his nightshirt, barefoot, he jumped over two walls, from one of which he almost fell into a well, and ran off to Riverou's house, where he caught up with the companions on the march. They were quite surprised to see a man all in white running and yelling after them, and crying because his feet were bleeding. Captain Saint-Lo, after threatening to make him return, pulled him up on the rump of his horse and gave him a filthy old cloak to sit on because the harness buckles were rubbing his bottom raw.

One league from there, at the ford at Reaux, this troop encountered a company of papists marching on Angoulême. They were scattered after a short skirmish in which the new soldier, still in shirtsleeves, won for himself a harquebus and some worn equipment. But he did not take any clothing even though necessity and his companions counseled him to do so. In this condition he arrived at the rendezvous in

Jonzac, where some officers had him properly armed and dressed. He wrote at the end of his enlistment agreement, ". . . stipulating that I shall never blame the war for impoverishing me, since I cannot possibly come out of it more poorly furnished than when I began."

The rendezvous for all the troops was at Saintes, where the governor, Monsieur de Mirambeau, pressed by [d'Aubigné's] relatives, wanted to send him home, first with arguments, then with orders. But the companion showed him no respect and, having given as a reason that he was on duty, walked away from the said lord and from his captain, Soubrand, who had agreed to detain him. He made his way through the whole company and fled. Then, holding a sword at the throat of one of his cousins, who had followed him, he went to the quarters of Captain Anières, whom he knew was quarreling with the sieur de Mirambeau. The next day, when a fight broke out between them, he was the first to set his match, and he almost killed his cousin, who was in Mirambeau's party.[20]

One evening that winter, which was very cold, Anière's company was positioned in front of the enemy along the edge of a frozen swamp. In the mud and far from their fires the men were chilled to the bone. An old sergeant, Dauphin, came along to light the match for our young man. Seeing him trembling, he offered him his scarf, which the frozen fellow joyfully accepted.

But his worst times that winter were in Perigord with the regiment of Piles, and his return from the siege of Angoulême, where he joined in the attack on the park and won for himself a new outfit in the city. But [retreating from there] along the road to Pons, he was so exhausted that he could only crawl by night from one peasant hearth to another. When he rejoined his company the next morning he heard men foraging all around. Despite his miseries he turned away when he saw his well-mounted cousins ride by, for he feared their taunts.

In Pons he joined the attack on the city and helped in its capture. There he avenged one of his aunts, whom a Captain Banchereau had tried to rape.[21] He also fought in skirmishes around Jazeneuil, in the battle of Jarnac, and in the big fight at La Rocheabeille; but he missed the battle of Moncontour because he had retreated with the men from his own region.[22] Even so, he ran no less risk than if he had been in that battle because he was with the sieur de Savignac who led the action that you can find described in the first tome of the *Histoire*:

[Savignac had led a force of some eighty cavalry commanded by himself and two other captains on a foray in the direction of Libourne. After some initial successes they were severely mauled in a night attack.] Of the eighty soldiers only five survived, namely the three captains whom we have listed, one common soldier, and the commanding officer. The three captains had escaped [the night attack] because they had been on guard, having been unable to coax this duty from their exhausted men. Savignac had been paralyzed from the thighs down and had not walked for ten years; his courage alone made him mount a horse and try to fight. But this time, he was so frightened that he managed to run away at top speed. (*Histoire*, 5.16.115)

[D'Aubigné] did not want to put in his book that he was himself so frightened that night that, recalling his insolence with his kinsmen, he prayed earnestly to God, saying in self-accusation, "The untamed will be tamed by the evils, etc."[23]

[In flight from that rout and heading toward Coutras] he crossed the river Dronne with the help of a peasant who had come to kill him. Against all odds, his horse managed to cross after him, and with great effort they pulled it from the mud. They crossed the Isle at Laubardement, and his guide led him right up to the gate of the city of Coutras but did not dare go farther. It should be noted in passing that later in the house of Savignac this same peasant, whose name was Peirot de Fargue, was brought in before d'Aubigné, who identified him from among six who were present, so well does fear keep her records. From the entrance to Coutras d'Aubigné made his way along a street and came to the docks on the river, where he stopped to consider how he might get across. He saw running toward him from the direction of the mill four harquebusiers who were making ready to fire at him, and several others who were following close behind. That made him jump into the river without further thought, and he began to swim, holding one of his pistols that he had not yet fired up out of the water. When he found some footing he got across in spite of those who were shooting at him in the water and others who ran toward him along the bank. The dangers that he risked in that adventure still can make themselves felt, as you will see elsewhere.[24]

But all of this did not correct him. To give you an example of his willful independence: one day, among five hundred harquebusiers passing in review before the prince of Condé, he called those who took off their hats *bisognes*.[25] The prince, observing this and learning who he was, wished to offer him a place in his own household. This honor was told him by Monsieur de La Caze, who said something to the effect that he wanted to give him to the prince. His brash answer was: "Stick to giving your dogs and your horses." This is a second example I note for you of his rude independence.

He spent the rest of the third war in Saintonge and was present at the defeat of two Italian companies and of two others commanded by L'Herbette at Jonzac. And there for the first time he was trusted to lead twenty harquebusiers, *enfants perdus*.[26] The high and well-positioned barricade was strongly defended, and was forced only by the heroics of Boisrond.[27]

Clermont d'Amboise, Ranti, and others, having retreated into Archiac, were attacked several times by La Rivière-Puitaillé, who was based in Pons with five Italian and four French cavalry troops. Some fine engagements were fought in which the guardsmen of [the Huguenot captain] D'Acier taught the Saintongeois a few lessons. There d'Aubigné had the honor to accept a horseman's challenge, and he shot him at such close range that he knocked him to the ground. After that he turned down a number of commands but held out for (and later obtained) that of the first company.

Archiac was put under siege when he was in Cognac, but he managed to get into the city and to bring soldiers carrying powder. One of them, who insisted on carrying the match, set fire to his pack and got off with the loss of his sight.

Anière's ensign Blanchard, since known as Cluseau, and he led the *enfants perdus* to the siege of Cognac, where they were rudely received by the soldiers in the market hall. The action became quite lively, especially for d'Aubigné, who, in his doublet, attacked the barricade at the end of the draw bridge, throwing off a cupboard and two chests and pushing forward, not without the loss of some good men for this folly. Anière honored him for it by having him receive the capitulation. In this action one gentleman was trapped when the drawbridge was raised, and he was not released until the surrender. As for the last action in that war, you can read about his capture of Pons at the end of the twenty-eighth chapter of the fifth book.[28]

But it must yet be added that on our return from there, while the peace was being negotiated, Anière's regiment was marching with a great deal of fear around Royon. There our new ensign, in command of thirty mounted harquebusiers, came upon the baron of La Garde, who was moving up to attack the regiment. He made such a bold face before the enemy that he drew the attack upon himself and thus saved his companions. But two hours later a continuous fever put him to bed. Then and there, thinking that he was about to die, he made the hair of the captains and of the others who had come to see him stand on end when he confessed his sins, having mainly on his conscience the pillaging forays on which he had led his men, and especially for not having seen to the punishment of the soldier Auvergnac, who had killed an old peasant for no reason. And there he clearly showed his mistake in having dared to assume command before age had given him the authority for it. That illness changed him completely and restored his true character.[29]

TWO

✳

A Mistress and a Master

1570-1576

When the peace for the third war had been signed, his guardian gave him a little money and a lease on his property at Les Landes as the only titles.[1] With that, and accompanied by an intermittent fever, he arrived in Blois, where he found that a steward of the duke of Longueville had made himself his heir, was enjoying his wealth, and therefore, judging him an impostor, offered to prove to him that d'Aubigné had been killed in Savignac's charge, for which he had attestations. The young man took this reception and his other troubles so to heart that, after seeking out his maternal relatives in the Blésois, all of whom turned their backs on him out of hatred for his religion, his misery left him no other hope than for death. In the fury of his fever he predicted that one day they would all pay him homage. His farmer came to see him and recognized him by a plague sore that he had had from the pestilence in Orleans; but seeing him in such a sorry state and without a sign of life, the wretch rallied to the false heirs for fear of having to pay three years of rent at once. With this the piteous young man, abandoned by relatives, wealth, and fortune, had himself taken half-dead to Orleans by boat, and there carried into

18

the courtroom, where, seated on a low chair, he was allowed to plead his case. His exordium was so pathetic, and so well supported by his pitiful state, that the judge looked with anger at his adversaries. Thereupon they rose up, exclaimed that no one but the son of d'Aubigné could speak like that, and begged his forgiveness.

Having his bit of wealth now in his hands he fell in love with Diane Salviati, the eldest daughter of Talcy. This love inspired him to write some poetry in French, and he composed what we call his *Printemps*, in which there are many harsh passages but also a kind of fury that many will like.[2]

The campaign around Mons in Hainaut began, and he was raising a company for it.[3] He was in Paris at the time of the royal wedding to get his commission when, serving as a second in a duel near the Place Maubert, he wounded a sergeant who tried to arrest him.[4] For that he had to leave Paris, and the Saint Bartholomew massacre began three days later.[5]

I want to give an example of what God reserves to Himself when it comes to courage: when he learned of the massacre d'Aubigné and eighty of his men, among whom you could easily choose a dozen of the boldest soldiers of France, were wandering about in the countryside without any clear purpose. When, without reason or design, a voice cried out, "There they are!" they ran off like a flock of sheep, losing their breath before they lost their fear. Then, in groups of three or four, holding each other's hands, each witness to the mettle of his fellows, they looked at themselves covered with shame and avowed that God does not give, but only lends, bravery and understanding. The next day half of them went forth to meet six hundred killers coming down the Loire from Orleans and Beaugency. They waited behind the levee until a good number had landed. When they were discovered they attacked, driving the enemy back to their boats, killing many, and thus saving Mer from pillage.

D'Aubigné, withdrawing to Talcy, sent forty of his men to Sancerre, reserving himself for La Rochelle along with those of his men who preferred to fight there.[6] In the meantime he hid out at Talcy, where one day, recounting his troubles to the father of his mistress, he told how his means did not permit him to return to La Rochelle. The old man replied, "You told me once that the original documents concerning the enterprise at Amboise had been entrusted to your father, and also that on one of the papers there was the seal of the Chancellor L'Hospital who now is retired at his home near Etampes.[7] He is a man who is no longer useful and who has disavowed your party. If you let me send a man to advise him that you possess this document, I take it upon myself to get you ten thousand crowns, either from him, or from those who will use the [document] against him." At these words d'Aubigné went to get a pouch of faded velvet, showed the documents, and after thinking about them threw them into the fire. When the lord of Talcy saw this he chided him. His reply was, "I burned them lest they burn me, for I had considered the temptation." The next day this good fellow took the suitor by the hand with these words: "While you have not yet let me know all your thoughts, I am not so blind that I cannot see that you love my daughter. You know that she is sought by several who are wealthier than you." This being conceded, he continued. "Those papers that you burned so they wouldn't burn you, they have warmed me, and I can tell you that I wish you for a son." D'Aubigné answered, "Monsieur, for having rejected a mean and ill-gotten treasure, you give me another that I cannot begin to measure."

Some days later in a village in Beauce, d'Aubigné was

dismounting at the gate of an inn when he was attacked and almost killed by a horseman who had followed him. D'Aubigné grabbed a sword from a kitchen boy and, in slippers, ran out to meet the other who had turned around to attack again. A blow from the horse's head jolted the man on foot and stunned him. But he recovered and thrust the sword against the body of the horseman, whom he found to be in armor. Striking again, he gave him a half-foot of blade through a gap in the cuirass, then slipped on the ice as he tried to jump aside. The other lost no time pulling him up and he stabbed him twice, once deeply in the head. The wounded man hurled himself at the other and grasped him about the body, but the horse pulled back and left him sprawled on the ground. He could see from the dubious look of the surgeon that his wounds were grievous. Without even letting anyone change the original dressings on the wounds he left before dawn, because he wanted to die in the arms of his mistress. The exhausting ride of twenty-two leagues caused a hemorrhage of all his blood, and he arrived without feeling, sight, or pulse. He lay without dressings or food for two days. Finally, with a bit of nourishment he began to show signs of life. And they concluded about him that without this change of blood he could never have lived with himself because of the hot temper that ruled him.[8]

His relatives had the bishop of Orleans send his procurator with six officers of justice to force the sieur de Talcy to surrender his guest to them, but they could get nothing but equivocal answers to their questions and so they turned back. Since the members of [Salviati's] household had refused to provide an attestation [as to d'Aubigné's whereabouts] the procurator went away threatening to destroy the house. D'Aubigné mounts a horse, catches up with the company two leagues away, and, with his pistol clenched in his teeth, makes the procurator abjure all the articles of faith of the papacy. The wretch redeemed his disgrace by forging his own attestation on the road back.

Love and poverty had kept d'Aubigné from rushing back to La Rochelle. Now the chevalier Salviati broke off the marriage agreement because of the difference of religion.[9] D'Aubigné's anguish was such that he fell into an illness so severe that several physicians came from Paris to care for him, among them Postel, who, after urging his patient to make his last confession, stayed to guard him from being murdered.[10]

After the Peace of La Rochelle was signed and the intrigues of Monsieur and of the king of Navarre began,[11] one of the latter's stewards, Estounau, reminded his master of the services of the late sieur d'Aubigné and advised him to make use of the son as a man who found nothing too hot to handle. This arrangement was conducted in secret, at the time the war in Normandy began.[12] Because the prisoner-king was held under very close surveillance he wanted d'Aubigné to make a trip with Fervacques, at that time a great enemy of the Huguenots, as if he himself had sent him.[13] Moreover, Poupelinière and a minister from Normandy suggested to d'Aubigné that he could try to save Count Montgomery, something he could in conscience do provided he swore no oath. You can see what he did about all this under the titles "Guidon of Fervacques" and "Squire of the King of Navarre" in book 7, chapter 7.[14]

The king of Navarre, advised of these matters, recalled his young man to the court just before the death of King Charles.[15] D'Aubigné, who wanted to see the death of the king, was observed by the queen as she was leaving the royal chamber. She had been warned of his presence by Matignon, who hated d'Aubigné for having put a pistol to his head.

Moreover, in the mind of the queen he was a criminal because of his name. She assailed him now, reproaching him for the news she had heard of his activities in Normandy and for the fact that he resembled his father. The gallant could only reply to that, "May God be so good to me." He saw by the anger on her face that she, accompanied as she was only by Lansac, needed a captain of the guard to arrest him, and so he beat a hasty retreat. He would have had to leave the court completely but for the skill of his master [in protecting him]. And Fervacques on his return answered for his guidon by denying everything, and didn't leave him at court but took him along with the other officers of the prisoner-king of Navarre. That explains how he was present at the capture of Archecourt in Germany, which he was the first to enter, at the fight for the bridge over the Aisne, and at the battle of Dormans the next day, all of this without yet swearing any oath for the desire he had to save Montgomery.[16] In this last melee, where he charged thirty paces ahead of the line, he didn't manage to take prisoner any leader except for a gentleman from Champagne named De Verger, who begged him to accept a ransom. He refused it, even though he didn't have a crown, as well as the offer of a horse, although his own was wounded in the head. Instead, he simply quoted to his prisoner:

> Helas! combien m'est ennuyeuse
> Ceste demeure mal'heureuse . . .
>
> [Alas! how painful is to me
> This dwelling where I chance to be]

with the rest of the stanza.

This campaign made d'Aubigné a familiar of Monsieur de Guise, which did not hurt his position at court and which fostered a more important friendship between his master and the duke. These two princes slept, ate, and performed together in the masques, ballets, and carousings of which d'Aubigné alone was the organizer. About that time he planned to produce the *Circe*, which the queen mother rejected because of the cost. King Henry III has since produced it for the wedding of the duke of Joyeuse.[17]

He made himself known among the ladies of the court with his quips and banter. One day, for example, when he was sitting alone on a bench three ladies-in-waiting to the queen, Boudeilles, Beaulieu, and Tenie, who all together must have added up to 140 years, sensing that he was new to the court, looked him over closely. Then one of the three asked him boldly, "What are you looking at there, Monsieur?" this in a harsh tone. He replied in kind. "At the antiques of the court, Mesdames." These ladies, embarrassed, went on to seek his friendship and an offensive and defensive alliance. This kind of impudence, and there was more, put him on intimate terms with the ladies. And then there were the fights: an attack he and three others once made against thirty idlers, for the most part pikemen; another to save the children of the marquis de Tran pursued by thirty men; another against the guards of the maréchal de Montmorency, who had trapped Fervacques in the Chapeau Rouge;[18] another fight when he and Fervacques, with a page and some valets, were jumped by thirteen thieves in chain mail and steel caps, and the two of them were wounded; other attacks made on the horseguards with Bussy. He became great friends with this cavalier after serving as a second for Fervacques, who had a duel with him.[19] And in his wilder moments he would lead a few of the young lords of the court like the count of Gurson, Sagonne, Pequigny, and others out at night to challenge the city guard, and then slip back into the palace by a different door. In this sport our companion was finally caught at the barrier at Saint-Jacques-de-la-Boucherie along with a few men they had called to for help. He was wounded and, as he was being led away, he managed to free his sword, clear a passage, and make his escape.

In a tournament in which the king of Navarre, two of the Guisards, and the squire of the king appeared, Diane de Talcy was present. She was at that time promised to Limeux, her first engagement having been broken because of religion. This demoiselle, hearing and seeing by the esteem of the court the difference between what she had lost and what she possessed, fell into a depression from which she became ill and never recovered.

The queen mother scolded her son-in-law because Falesche, his first steward, and his squires were not going to mass. To check up on that, one Tuesday after Easter as the princes were playing handball, the king of Navarre asked d'Aubigné, who had just arrived in the gallery, if he had made his Easter duty. He, taken by surprise, replied, "What's that, Sire?" The question was repeated with, "and on which day?" He answered, "Friday," not knowing that there was but that one poor day in the whole year without a mass. Monsieur de Guise observed in a loud voice that he obviously had not been well catechised, and all the princes began to laugh. But not the queen, who had him watched even more closely.

At that time the queen had twenty or thirty spies, almost all renegades. One of them, named Le Buisson, had tried to suborn the elder Dangeau in order to entrap the duke of Guise. When d'Aubigné found out how this gallant was trying to destroy a man of good family, he told Fervacques about it in Lyons. The latter advised him to kill him in a little street where [Le Buisson] frequently brought Dangeau to plot their actions. This would have been done, except that

Nambut was killed in the same place for a similar reason just as Le Buisson appeared for his own ambush.

It happened after that that d'Aubigné, with his usual Gallic candor, rebuked Lady Carnavalet for her incestuous liaison with Fervacques and for poisoning her mother, the countess of Morevert.[20] Fervacques swore to have him killed. To carry this out, with risk only to others, he informed the duke of Guise that Le Buisson, who was in his service, and Dangeau wanted to betray and entrap the duke, and that d'Aubigné was with them, even though the latter knew what Le Buisson was about. D'Aubigné, thus compromised, went to see the duke as he was preparing for bed. He offered to maintain what Fervacques had said if the duke would be good enough to lock him in the handball court with the traitor, who [was in fact present and who] from the beginning of the talk had been clutching the knob of a chair. But the duke of Guise was too prudent for that and instead sent Le Buisson out to see what was going on in the Louvre. Then he said, "D'Aubigné, my friend, it is not with a sword and a dagger that you can hope to straighten out this affair. That would mean fighting the queen. He is involved in a business that you do not understand, but he will never again eat at my table."[21] It was clear that this prince added much friendship to his judgment.

Some days later Fervacques, still wanting to keep the promise he had made to his cousin to kill her informer, pretended one night that he was despondent. He begged d'Aubigné to go walking with him behind the Couture Sainte-Catherine, but he aroused a bit of suspicion when he tried too deliberately to keep him from taking along a dagger that his lackey carried. When they came to a little bridge, which has since been changed, Fervacques began to talk like this: "My friend, being resolved to quit this world, I regret nothing in it but you. I have come here to kill myself. Give me an embrace and I will die content." D'Aubigné, backing off, said, "Monsieur, you told me once that the greatest comfort you could find when you were about to die would be to take along, with a thrust of your dagger, the best of your friends. My advice is not to die, especially for a person whose cut and material are worth so little. So let's not embrace on it." Immediately, Fervacques draws his sword and dagger and with head down charges at d'Aubigné, cursing God, and saying, "Because you defy me we will die together." "No, just you," says the other, "if I can manage it." And backing up a few steps he put himself on guard and held Fervacques at bay. Then the latter threw down his sword and dagger, fell to his knees, cried that he was out of his mind, and begged his opponent to kill him. This being refused, they separated. But d'Aubigné was naive to think that they were reconciled, for a few days later Fervacques poisoned his soup, which made his bowels move eighty times in one day, his hair fall out, and his skin peel. Not until long after did he learn from a physician named Stellatus, who had treated him in that misfortune, that Fervacques had threatened to kill him if he revealed [to d'Aubigné] that poison was the cause. Later, when [Fervacques] was refused the governorship of Normandy, he took it into his head to join the king of Navarre. He missed no kind of flattery to reconcile himself with d'Aubigné, who at that time was in the fullest confidence of his prince. From all of this came the deliberations [to attempt an escape] that you can find recounted in book 7, chapter 20 of the *Histoire*.[22]

Here are some private details not worthy of the *Histoire*: the king of Navarre stopped for a bite to eat in a village near Montfort-L'Amaury, where, feeling the need to relieve himself, he made use of a hamper. An old woman came upon him as he sat there and would have split his skull with a billhook but for d'Aubigné, who later said to his master to make him laugh, "If you had had so honorable a death I would have composed an epitaph for you in the Saints-Innocents style."[23] It would go:

> Cy gist un Roy par grande merveille,
> Qui mourut, comme Dieu permet,
> D'un coup de serpe, et d'une vieille,
> Comme il chioit dans une met.

> [Here lies a king, o wondrous end,
> Who died, as God permitted,
> Of a billhook thrown by an aged crone,
> As in her hutch he shitted.]

He had another opportunity to laugh that day when a gentleman, seeing our troop approach his village, came riding out, thrashing his horse in his haste to turn us away. But he had trouble deciding who was our leader, and finally settled on Rocquelaure, who had the most gold lace. We spared his village on condition that he guide us to Châteauneuf, which we only did to keep him from spreading news of our passage around the countryside. He entertained the king with gossip from the royal court, especially about the princesses, among whom he did not spare the queen of Navarre. That night, arriving at the docks of Châteauneuf, it happened that Frontenac said to Captain L'Espine, the prince's chamberlain, who spoke to us from the top of the wall, "Open for your master." Our gentleman knew to whom Châteauneuf belonged, and he became very frightened. D'Aubigné had him take a back road to escape, and he didn't get home for three days.

The king of Navarre reached Saumur by way of Alençon. Since he had not yet made a profession of his religion no one participated in the communion service except La Rocque and d'Aubigné.[24] When Laverdin arrived, he and d'Aubigné went off to the fighting in Maine, from where he brought back the colors of Saint-Phal; then he enticed thirty more gallants away from the court, and got into the fighting and affairs described in chapter 21 of said book.[25]

From there the king of Navarre made his journey into Gascony, where Fervacques made several attempts on d'Aubigné's life. Even when he learned that he couldn't stay in the service of this prince and was dismissed, he remained for some three months just to carry out his vengeance. At about that time began the love affair between the king and young Tignonville who, as long as she remained unmarried, resisted him virtuously.[26] The king wanted to use d'Aubigné [in that affair] because he had learned that for him nothing was impossible. But the latter, roguish enough in big enterprises, and perhaps even willing to provide such service for a companion as a prank, balked at the name and role of pimp, which he called a beggar's vice, and the exaggerated pleadings and snivelling appeals of his master, who even got down on his knees with hands clasped, could not move him. The prince then changed his tactics and used the quarrel with Fervacques to make himself indispensable, like one day when he said to d'Aubigné before a number of people, "Fervacques says that he did not commit the treason that you have alleged, and that he will fight you to prove it." The reply was, "He could not have found a more honorable man to bring me this message. And I have had the honor of serving under his colors. Therefore, I will touch my hat before I will touch my sword." When the king insisted on a reconciliation, d'Aubigné reminded him of the oath of hatred that they all swore when he kissed the cheeks of his companions.[27]

On passing through Poitou a lute player named Tougiras, who had served [d'Aubigné's] father and who was then in the service of La Boulaye, brought him some inside information picked up by [the latter] and by his cousin Saint-Gelais.[28] As a result of this information the two of them invited some other lords and gentlemen, like Montdion, Berteauville, and others, to join them behind trunks and in wardrobes and wait for d'Aubigné until one hour after midnight, and then to accompany him to an ambush that Fervacques had prepared. The plot had been discovered one evening in Lectoure when the intended victim, returning home alone, found Saquenay, a Burgundian gentleman in Fervacques's service, waiting for him at a corner of the street with two pistols cocked and loaded, and the [guard] dog killed. D'Aubigné jumped at his throat so quickly that he tore away his pistols, but he did him no other harm, because Saquenay, whom he had once led in battle, swore that he was there against his will. And he revealed other schemes of Fervacques, who, when all had failed, finally withdrew from the court. But before leaving he said to Fecquières, maid of honor to Madame,[29] that his heart grieved for the wicked things that he had done to his old friend and that he wanted to bid him adieu and beg his forgiveness. D'Aubigné ran to the scoundrel's house to accommodate this good intention; but as he stepped up to his room, La Rocque, who was coming out, made him turn around most quickly, explaining, "He gave you this bait and is only waiting so he can kill you before he leaves."

After that d'Aubigné's favor with the king declined. When his friends realized this they repeatedly urged him to yield a little in accommodating the pleasures of his master. One day, for example, Fonlebon and another [gentleman] pursued this argument during a full six leagues of riding.

They pointed out that the papists, being more indulgent, would win the heart of their master through his pleasures, which would prove most harmful to the religion and to the churches. The sieur de la Personne reminded him of the excellence of his eloquence in speech, verse, and prose, and his talents for the niceties of court life, saying and concluding that he should use these gifts to win his master's favor. D'Aubigné dismounted and faced them to answer. To the first: "You are saying then that I must close my eyes to evil for the good of the church; and you, that God has given me great talents and graces to make of me a pimp."

The king of Navarre, insistent in his determination but judging that the point of honor turned to d'Aubigné because of his stubborn integrity, made use of what happened one night when he almost had to draw his sword to beat off hoodlums in the street and it was d'Aubigné who threw himself in front of the king and chased them off. After that he would take d'Aubigné along on his nightly escapades and the next day tell the ministers and the great lords of the party all about it. Malice prompted him to foment other kinds of trouble, too, to hold back his pay, and even to soil his clothing so as to reduce him to the most dire need.

THREE

∗

Into Action and Out of Favor

1576-1579

[D'Aubigné] was sent to prepare the provinces and governments of Guyenne, Perigord, Saintonge, Angoumois, Aunis, Poitou, Anjou, Touraine, Maine, Perche, Beauce, Ile-de-France, Normandy, and Picardy for war, and to seek out some dangerous information in Artois.[1] No sooner had he been dispatched than the queen mother was informed, and she set many traps for him, as you can find described at the end of the fourth chapter, book 8:

[One of the traps was set in Blois, where d'Aubigné went for the opening of the States General in December 1576 in order to learn the views of the delegates. Although he was recognized, he was still determined] to carry out his mission . . . and he made sure he appeared, even though it was known that he had provided the king of Navarre not only with the means but also the desire to escape from the court. As he stood among the young gallants, Vitry, a maid of honor to the queen, left her place and came to warn him that he should leave. She pointed out Magnane, lieutenant of the guard, and La Bonde, the officer who had just been given orders to arrest him. [d'Aubigné], laughing and joking with Vitry, suddenly slipped behind their majesties and from there through the private rooms of the queen, and made his way to a corner of the garden, where he changed clothing with his valet. He then went out among the servants of Fontenilles, and on to the livery at Fois where he found Quergrois, who, seeing no harm in it, gave him a boat. (*Histoire*, 8.4.128)

We will add only that while he was in Blois he wrote the speech that the Baron of Mirambeau delivered.[2]

When he had finished his mission [and was returning to report to the king] he encountered a troop of gentlemen who were marching to Saint-Gelais with a plan to attack Niort. He let himself be taken prisoner so as to be sure of finding his friend Saint-Gelais, and he was delivered by Van-sai's men at the very time that Monsieur de Damville was marching to negotiate with the kings. Saint-Gelais gave his prisoner a troop of light horse to lead; [with them] he attacked the Saint-Gelais gate wearing only a doublet, and got his coat scorched by a harquebus shot.[3]

Back in Gascony he and La Noue[4] led the reckless charge that you can find described in the eighth chapter of the same book, attributed to Vachonière's lieutenant.

[At the siege of Marmande, January 1577] La Noue summoned Vachonière's lieutenant and had him select twelve men from his light cavalry troop. With him, and Du Busas and his brother, they numbered in all fifteen horsemen. He ordered them not to arm themselves yet nor to charge, but first studied the situation . . . ; then] Vachonière's lieutenant crept close to the embankment under the wall and noted a carrier's path which extended out from the wall like a ridge and which would permit them to get close to the defenders. He reported this to La Noue, who ordered them to attack. The troop rode down through the moat and came out by the ridge, where the defenders fled suddenly in terror. His men took a harquebus volley fired down on them by the defenders on the wall, then they charged. Two-thirds of the enemy jumped down into the ditch on the other side of the wall, but the rest seized their swords and met the charge, supported by four or five captains and seven or eight sergeants armed with pikes and halberds. But the horsemen attacked furiously and made them follow the others over the wall, except for thirty who lay where they had fallen. La Noue brought back two of his men who had been killed and almost all the others, many with wounds. He himself had six harquebus wounds, one behind the ear. If you find this attack told in unusual detail, the reason is that it was considered the most reckless of all those led by that most headstrong leader of his time. (*Histoire*, 8.8.172–173)

Only you should know two of his vanities that are unworthy of the *Histoire*: one, when he saw that he was the only man in his troop who was wearing brassards, he took them off before the attack; the other, in the heat of combat he saw that a bracelet he wore on his left arm with a lock of his mistress's hair in it had caught fire from a harquebus shot; he put his sword in his left hand to save the bracelet [with his right]. Captain Bourget, with whom he contested that day among others, called out that he had seen that gesture and, to prove a similar coolness under fire, pointed out an orb and a cross that decorated his sword. After these dangers he did not hesitate to risk some more at Saint Macaire; you will find it described at some length at the end of the same chapter.

[Saint Macaire was a town on the Garonne defended by a castle set on rock that rises thirty feet above the river. The ramparts on that side were an additional eighteen feet high. Despite this barrier, an assault from the river was decided and a force of 260 men embarked in small boats.] A sentinel called out as they approached. To his "Who goes there?" we answered, "Wheat." But he gave the alarm when he saw that our cargo was men and ladders. Genissac and Serrouette took one ladder, Vachonière's lieutenant and Castera the other. They scurried up on the rock and set their ladders against the wall. Even though the ladders were too short to reach the parapet, the men clambered up. The windows of the castle and of an adjoining house soon filled with defenders. Vachonière's lieutenant received the first harquebus shot, then Captain More knocked him from the ladder with a board. He found himself rolling down the rock to the water's edge with his pistol still up on the wall. Castera took his place on the ladder, as Serrouette followed Genissac, who was knocked off by a harquebus shot. The fury of the attackers was such that they continued the assault although they were under fire from all sides. If the ladders had been longer they would have been safer inside the walls than retreating to their boats. But they finally had to retreat and lost even more men, among others Guerci killed by a barrel dropped on him by a woman on the wall. The king of Navarre's guards retreated to another rock, where, on the assurance that they were really Catholic, they were taken prisoner. Half of the men who reached the boats were killed, and everyone would have been lost but for La Cassaigne, who, despite a shattered arm, managed to work an oar and to push off into the river. From that action there were only twelve men who were not killed, wounded, or taken prisoner . . . (*Histoire*, 8.8.185–187)

His pursuit of danger and glory at every opportunity added envy to the anger of his master. In the meantime, however, this prince was becoming concerned with the state of affairs in Languedoc. D'Aubigné was sent there and brought the negotiations to an end, as you can see described at length in the eighth chapter of the same book, and he ran many risks on his return. Being a zealous partisan he made a big mistake when he got back, for he was not supposed to reveal the names of the traitors, even to La Noue, to whom he reported, but was to pass them to the knowledge of his master alone, as you will find in the fourteenth chapter of the same book.[5]

At this point I would like to state clearly that d'Aubigné,

learning of the decision to have him killed and thrown in the river, caught his master one day at supper and in full company spoke to him as follows: "So, my lord, you have been able to plan the death of the man whom God has chosen as the guide for your life, a service for which I make no objection, any more than I do for my skin all pierced [by wounds], but rather to have served you without your having made of me a flatterer or a pimp. May God forgive you the death which you seek to cause. You can tell from the way in which I address you how much I wish to hasten it." There followed so much bitterness that the king left the table. You can take all this as a lesson to avoid being so outspoken.

We have also not explained in the *Histoire* that d'Aubigné, still recovering from an eight-day fever, had chosen because of his weakness a dagger for one hand and a pistol for the other as weapons for a duel.[6] The affair was broken up, however, and his friends advised him to leave the court, which he did by going to Castel-Jaloux, where he had a commission.[7] It is worth noting that several gentlemen of the court of Navarre, with Constans, Sainte-Marie, and Arambure taking the lead, accompanied him when he went to bid adieu to his master, who was returning from a ride, and they did not bother to dismount. When [d'Aubigné] arrived in Castel-Jaloux he wrote to Laverdin in these terms: "Monsieur, I would like to remind you that I was willing, against all kinds of advice, to meet you, having accepted your word that the challenge was mine to you alone; now, however doubtful may be, if not your honor, at least your precautions, [let me say that] if the lord of La Magdaleine is still willing to back you with his sword,[8] there are many open fields between here and Nerac in any of which I will meet you at the time and place you wish, without need for other pledges."

After that there took place the dreadful fight that you can find described in the same chapter 14:

[Four days after his arrival in Castel-Jaloux, d'Aubigné accompanied the town commander, Vachonière, and a small force of Huguenot cavalry and infantry in an expedition against Marmande. They found there a far superior royalist garrison and had to beat a hasty retreat. But good order was not maintained, and a number of scattered fights ensued. One of these took place along a narrow roadway lined by hedgerows from which harquebusiers could fire on the retreating men, and where the horsemen fought each other at such close quarters] that the heads of our horses reached over the saddles of our foes.

Vachonière, his back broken by chained balls and smoking from four harquebus shots, trapped on the ground between the legs of his lieutenant's horse, begged the latter to save himself. But soon they were both on the ground and covered by the bodies of three of their men. It was like fighting against a wall: they couldn't move.

The elder Borcas and D'Aiguillon were at each other's throat with daggers. Bacoue and his man were doing the same in a ditch, except that Bacoue was finished off by pikemen who had come up through the ditches. As the Protestants backed off, Dominge saw that the lieutenant, whom they had left for dead, had managed to free himself from one of the bodies lying on him and, still on the ground, to wield his sword with his right arm, protected by the horses milling about him and by the wounds he managed to inflict on Metaut, Bastanes, and young Mège, who died of his. Dominge then rallied young Castain and two others and these four pulled him free and put him on the first horse they could catch. A hundred paces away they turned to face the elder Mège and others who were in pursuit. They crossed swords again, but did not stay because the main force from Marmande was approaching, and also because the lieutenant was wounded in three places. (*Histoire*, 8.8.242–243)

On his return [from that fight] he was put to bed for his

wounds. The surgeons being doubtful about them, he dictated to the judge of the town the first lines of his *Tragiques*.

I shouldn't deny you a good example of the envy of princes. Young Bacoue went to Agen, where he was questioned by the king of Navarre about this battle.[9] He praised d'Aubigné lavishly, either because young men set no bounds to either praise or blame, or perhaps because he thought that he and his companions owed their lives to the man whose charges had paid for their mistakes. So, when he said that he had seen d'Aubigné thrust half the barrel of his pistol between the breastplate and the leather collar of Captain Metau before he fired, the king called him a liar. That was why [Bacoue] then wrote a letter to his relatives in Castel-Jaloux and asked them to tell what they knew of the fight. He showed their reply to Laverdin, who carried it to the king, adding that the two Mèges, Bastavets, and three others were still showing the wounds that [d'Aubigné] gave them when they tried to kill him on the ground. When Laverdin recounted all this to the king, the latter replied that Captain Dominge had been there and that he would be an honest witness. But it happened that this captain had vowed not to return to the court until he had won an action against the enemy. In the meantime, d'Aubigné recovered from his wounds and led his men into action around Bayonne, in the battle you can find described in chapter 15, book 8.

Dominge, having fulfilled his vow, went to Agen, where he found his master playing handball with Laverdin. They stopped their game to question him. He spoke of the action [at Castel-Jaloux] with praise for his captain, not as extravagant as that of Bacoue, but more judicious, and thereby completely lost the friendship of his master as well as compensation for thirty-eight harquebus wounds that he had suffered. Note what the great men of this world turn their backs to, even the best of them.

After the death of Vachonière the people of Castel- Jaloux wanted to have d'Aubigné appointed their governor, but he cut this off very quickly because he knew how poisoned were his prince's feelings for him. [Instead] he took by storm Castelnau-de-Mesme, a town on the road to Bordeaux. But the lady of the town insinuated herself into the bed and the good graces of Laverdin, and she easily persuaded the captors to renounce the capture, even though the sieurs de Meru and de La Noue, in the name of the party, were opposed, and the men from Castel-Jaloux were determined to keep up the war.[10] So the lady of Castelnau went to Bordeaux for help and got Admiral Villars to come with fourteen pieces of artillery and the promise of the king of Navarre that there would be no help [in support of resistance to him]. As the admiral was advancing on the town, d'Aubigné occupied it with fifty light cavalry and almost two hundred mounted harquebusiers. Once inside, they dismounted and had their horses led in again. This gave the appearance of so large a force that the admiral mistook it for a relief expedition [sent out] despite the king's promise, and he beat a hasty retreat toward Manciet.

Afterward a few soldiers of the garrison were suborned by Laverdin, who assured them that by obeying the orders of their colonel they could not be considered traitors. These orders were to lend a hand to La Sale de Ciron of the enemy party [who was going to try] to recapture the town. These soldiers went and reported all this to their own captain; and under his instructions he had them join in the attack. But he himself returned to the town that night and received the papists. In that action he was wounded, and forty-six of the attackers fell. The king of Navarre was so angry about this that he called for Castelnau's surrender himself, even though it was held for him, with the threat of four cannon. The reply was that they had already laughed off fourteen.

Shortly afterward the peace was signed, and d'Aubigné taking leave wrote a farewell to his master in these terms:[11]

Sire, your memory will reproach you with the twelve years of my service, the twelve wounds upon my breast; it will remind you of your prison, and that it was this hand which writes that opened the locks. It is a hand that has remained pure in your service, free of your favors and of the temptations from your enemies and from you. With this letter it commends you to God, to Whom I offer all my past services and vow all those yet to come, by which I shall ever try to make you understand that in losing me you have lost your most faithful servant, etc.

Passing through Agen to thank Madame de Roques, who had cared for him like a mother during his afflictions, he found near her house a big spaniel named Citron who used to sleep at the king's feet and sometimes between Frontenac and d'Aubigné. The poor animal, dying of hunger, came out to greet him. Deeply moved by this affection, he found a woman to take care of the dog, then composed and attached to his curly ruff the sonnet which follows:

> Le fidèle Citron qui couchoit autrefois
> Sur vostre lit sacré, couche ores sur la dure:
> C'est ce fidelle chien qui apprit de nature
> A faire des amys et des traistres le chois:
>   C'est luy qui les brigans effrayoit de sa voix,
> Et des dents les meurtriers; d'où vient donc qu'il
>   endure
> La faim, le froid, les coups, les desdains et l'injure
> Payement coustumier du service des Roys.
>   Sa fierté, sa beauté, sa jeunesse agréable

Le fit chérir de vous, mais il fut redoutable
A vos haineux, aux siens, pour sa dexterité.

    Courtisans, qui jettez vos desdaigneuses veues
Sur ce chien delaissé, mort de faim par les rues,
Attendez ce loyer de la fidélité.

[Good old Citron, who used to sleep on your honored bed, now must sleep on the hard floor; he learned by nature to distinguish friends from traitors;

It was he who frightened off thieves with his bark, and cutthroats with his teeth; why then does he suffer hunger, cold, blows, scorn and insults, the usual payment for the service of kings?

His pride, his looks, his joyful youth made him dear to you, but to your foes, and his, he was fearsome for his speed.

Courtiers, who cast scornful looks at this forlorn dog, dying of hunger in the streets, await the same wage for fidelity.]

The dog had to be taken to see the king the next day as he was passing through Agen. The king's color changed when he read the sonnet. But there is more: some time later, at a general assembly of the church in Sainte-Foy, the delegates from Languedoc asked the whereabouts of d'Aubigné, who had saved their province. At their request and with no disagreement the sieurs d'Yolet and de Pagezy were sent to this prince to ask on behalf of the churches what had become of so useful a servant of God. He answered that he still considered him his man and that he would give orders for his return. However, d'Aubigné's plans were to bid farewell to his friends in Poitou, to sell his property, and to enter the service of Duke Casimir. But it turned out otherwise because, arriving at Saint-Gelais and even before dismounting, he saw in a window Suzanne de Lezay of the house of Vivonne, with whom he fell so deeply in love that he found his Germany with the lords of Saint-Gelais and of La Boulaye.[12] They jumped at this opportunity to confide to him some projects they were both considering. But his new love was mixed with the strong need he felt for rest. Still, his desire to make himself necessary [to their plans] spurred him to miss no opportunity to earn the esteem of his friends and the regret of his ungrateful master.

Thus he went to scout around Nantes and was almost captured.[13] He made no more efforts to promote that plan, but he did get involved with the activities around Montaigu and Limoges, where he was summoned by the lords du Prinsay and du Bouchet, who sought in him, as they put it, not only the prowess but also the zeal of a Huguenot. Well, you can read about this in book 9, chapter 4, to which I will only add the prediction he made to those two poor devils, with their heads about to fall, of how many blows each would take.

[Prinsay and Bouchet were two fiery Huguenot gentlemen who, acting under instructions from La Boulaye, plotted with the military commander of Limoges, Le Mas, to take control of the city. D'Aubigné, called to lead the soldiers who would carry out the plan, and suspecting a trap, went alone to Limoges to learn what he could. He met Le Mas at an inn outside the city walls and invited him to walk with him on a tour of the fortifications. Le Mas demurred, but urged d'Aubigné to proceed alone.] So they separated by the gate and the visitor went down to the left, walking slowly, looking at everything with interest. He hadn't taken four hundred steps when a man stepped out from among the guards and began to follow him. Then, to allay suspicion, this man passed him and seemed to urinate against a garden gate. When the wary visitor reached the same spot and saw no wetness, he took it as evidence that he was being spied upon.

Then he did something that would seem to be inconsistent with any concern: he pulled out a tablet and began to make sketches of the city, or at least he gave the appearance of doing so. This was to show that he was making his tour reassured that he had not been discovered. In that way he returned to the inn where Le Mas joined him with cheerful talk and gestures. [Despite the merriment there was danger for d'Aubigné. Forty soldiers stood in readiness at the gate nearby, and in the inn there were four or five officers dressed in old clothes and pretending to be merchants. But d'Aubigné's apparent confidence reassured Le Mas, and he sent the "merchants" back into the city before the drawbridge was raised for the night.] The drawbridge had now been raised, and its bottom side looked more beautiful to him than the face of his beloved. He joked a little more with Le Mas, bemoaned the passage of time, and they agreed that he could leave to put the finishing touches to the plot. [D'Aubigné rode back to Prinsay and Bouchet, who greeted his suspicions with laughter, and only grudgingly agreed to proceed with caution. Then d'Aubigné left them.] When he was gone Prinsay and Bouchet recalled the words, the arguments, the gestures, and the familiar manners of Le Mas, and they began to scoff at the ungrateful suspicions of their master. . . . And so, despite their promise, they went to Limoges, to the same inn of the Three Swords and to the same room, where there soon arrived the same merchants and the same peddlers. Their fellow conspirator seized their swords, the merchants seized them by the collar. Their trial took two hours but, because it was Sunday, the execution was deferred until Monday morning, when they were beheaded. (*Histoire*, 9.4.371–380)

FOUR

*

Marriage amid War and Intrigue

1579-1583

The reproaches made by the churches on behalf of d'Aubigné and the sense of loss that the king began to feel at his absence made him reconsider [the banishment]. In addition, treachery was discovered among his enemies, and he began to fear that Duke Casimir might become the protector of the churches. And he missed the rousing tales that he liked to hear, and to tell. All of this persuaded the king to recall him in four successive letters, each of which was thrown into the fire on its arrival. And the holdout was not impressed either when he learned that the king, informed of the incident at Limoges and believing d'Aubigné a prisoner, had set aside his wife's jewelry to ransom him. But he was finally moved when told that the king, thinking that he had been beheaded, showed great sorrow and even missed a couple of meals.

La Boulaye was chatting one day with La Magdaleine about the latter's quarrel with d'Aubigné. La Magdaleine admitted that they had been put at odds for no good reason, but La Boulaye, young and impetuous, goaded him and offered to bring back his friend so they could fight. When d'Aubigné learned of this he welcomed such an *entrée* to the court of Navarre. He wrote to La Boulaye and asked him to give dinner and lodging to La Magdaleine so that they could each leave on the appointed morning and meet halfway on the road from Barbaste to Nerac with sword and dagger, but no armor. To make this rendezvous d'Aubigné traveled by post from Mer near Orleans to Castel-Jaloux, and from there sent on a lackey who returned to Barbaste with a message that the arrangements were made and that La Magdaleine would sleep at [La Boulaye's] house so as not to miss the assignation. [The next day] the other, having prayed and breakfasted well, rode out to the agreed-upon place where, after waiting half an hour, he saw two horsemen approaching. La Boulaye, galloping in the lead, shouted out from a distance, "Miracle and truce," because his man had come down with a heavy cold at midnight and was stiff in all his members. "There," said the companion, "is the result of my prayers." And as a matter of fact, some eight years later d'Aubigné found La Magdaleine at Montauban, armed with a sword and still riding stiffly. He sent Frontenac to him to learn if he was sufficiently recovered to wield the sword as well as he used to do. The answer was no. Frontenac returned to report this to his man, who was already waiting outside the city walls, against the advice of [his friends] Reniers and Favas. What provoked this kind of bravado was the great reputation of his foe, who had killed eight gentlemen without himself losing a drop of blood.

The young nobles of the court, who had formed a club for themselves, which they called the *Demogorgonistes* because they called the leader of their silliness *Demogorgon*, came out to greet the returning outcast.[1] And I must tell you here about a *valet de chambre* named De Cour, a pleasant and valiant man, whom d'Aubigné had given to the king. But despite the urgings of the king and of d'Aubigné himself he would not stay but insisted on following d'Aubigné in his adversities. Now that a reconciliation had been made De Cour had returned to the court eight days before his master. The king asked him where he came from; he answered "yes." And he kept saying "yes" whatever the question put to him. "That's because," he finally explained, "what banishes good men from the company of their king is not having always said 'yes.'"

D'Aubigné was received by the king with embraces and expiatory promises. The queen received him with great warmth, too, hoping to get from him what she didn't find. A short time later the king of Navarre, wanting to come to a decision on a war over the cities to be surrendered, only summoned for the deliberations the viscount of Turenne, Favas, Constans, and himself. Of these five, four were in love and, taking their love affairs as guides, they planned the war that you find described in chapter 5 of book 9.[2]

I have said that the action at Limoges provided the opportunity for reconciliation of the master and his servant. I invite you to read about it in its entirety, starting at the beginning of the aforesaid chapter, where there are some valuable instructions.[3] After that you will read about the resumption of fighting and, in chapter 6 to its end, of the capture of Montaigu where you will learn of other deeds and dangers of the man we are describing.[4] But most important, in the tenth chapter of the same book read carefully of the action at Blaye, where, if a mistake is to be admitted in the conduct of d'Aubigné, it will be that when he rejoined his men, who had already decided to withdraw, he should have taken better care of his ladders.[5] Note also his burst of vanity and his bold words, which God punished: "When the ladders were brought up d'Aubigné, who had taken a big white plume for his emblem and was swollen with vanity, jumped down into the moat, swore an oath, and shouted that he was the king of Blaye" (*Histoire*, 9.1.41). Words that cost him dearly when Pardaillon told the king of Navarre that he should never entrust a governorship to so reckless a man.

The count of La Rochefoucauld took Usson, the governor of Pons, to Nerac. D'Aubigné's friends told him that the latter had been telling of the action around Blaye to the disadvantage of the attacker. He therefore gathered together Laleu and three other gentlemen who had served with him in that affair and, at great risk, they rode the eight leagues from Montaigu to Nerac. When they arrived he begged the king to let him confront Usson about the report, which he then delivered from his own mouth, and Usson approved it word for word. And he was permitted to dispute with any who wished to change it. And because one of Usson's men got roughed up, a settlement had to be made, and after that a declaration from the king of Navarre that you will find among your father's papers and that you should keep as a title of honor.

This trip explains why d'Aubigné was in Nerac when the maréchal de Biron made his arrogant march around the city as told in the eleventh chapter. Finding a real epidemic of fear among the Huguenots of Gascony he remembered an old trick from Castel-Jaloux and did honor to the house [with a surprise attack on Biron's advance guard].[6] It seemed more impressive than it really was in the eyes of the princesses and of the others who were not in very good humor at that time. Returning from there with fifteen mounted harquebusiers from Castel-Jaloux, he was attacked by sixty light cavalry of La Hait near Cours. Our d'Aubigné deployed his men so well that only two were wounded, whereas the attackers lost three gentlemen. But they almost suffered a deep embarrassment later while riding among the vineyards of Saint-Preux near Jarnac: the five of them from Montaigu were proceeding around midnight along a narrow path when d'Aubigné saw approaching them some men on horseback, who, without pausing, attacked them with swords. It is certain that if his men, who only wanted to get through, could have escaped, they would have run away, because they were in the midst of four enemy garrisons and they had no support at all in the whole area. But it would have been shameful, because their assailants were only two priests and two other drunks who had left their sword belts at a tavern and had sworn to attack anything that moved, for which we taught them a proper lesson.

That year [1580] was spent at Montaigu with some nice little war games. The cavalry stationed there rode in three brigades, one under La Boulaye, the governor, the next under the sieur de Saint-Estienne, and the last, a little more than a third, under d'Aubigné. The first brigade was called the Albanians because they always had their asses in the saddle.[7] In one of their sorties they attacked Pelissonière, an ensign of the duke of Mayenne, who lost eight of his men and escaped with his arm broken by a pistol shot. In another action around Angers they defeated a company from the regiment of Des Bruyères. And still Montaigu remained under siege.

You will see in the fifteenth and sixteenth chapters [an account of] the planning and preparation up to the end [of the siege]. I will only add that the ten assaults made on Montaigu that year, in each of which rope and dagger played, were anticipated by the knowledge d'Aubigné had of physiognomy [because they involved tricks and deceit]. Also, that the thirty sallies, in a third of which there was fighting, were all led by d'Aubigné, except one in which

Saint-Estienne led his Bas-Poitevins out to match the feats of those who were called the Albanians, but they did no other good than add to his reputation. And you should know for the end of this account that the captain whom the count of Lude summoned was d'Aubigné, and that the actions described under a hidden name are his as well.[8]

After the peace he went to Libourne, where he found a court full of princes and the opportunity to deal with the matters that you can find in the second chapter of the tenth book.[9] I have but to add a bit of gallantry that I didn't dare include in the *Histoire*. One day the constable of Portugal was strolling with d'Aubigné along the bank of the River Dronne. He began to sigh deeply; he tore a piece of bark from a tree, for the sap was running at the time, and, with many sighs and Spanish words of sorrow for a lady, wrote what follows:

> Oceani foelix properas si flumen ad oras,
>> Littus et Hesperium tangere fata sinunt:
> Siste parum, et liquidas qui jam dissolvar in undas,
>> Me extinctum lachrymis ad vada nota feres;
> Sic poterit teneras quae exurit flamma medullas
>> Mersa tamen patriis vivere forsan aquis.

[O blessed river, if you rush to the sea and the fates allow you to reach the western shore, stop a moment that I, who soon will melt into your clear waters and die, might be borne like my tears to familiar shores; thus, the flame that burns my tender marrow will live again, submerged, in my father's sea.]

On his knees, melting into tears, he was about to throw it into the stream when d'Aubigné grasped his wrist, read the verses aloud, and thereupon translated on the same piece of bark the Latin hexastich into a lyric sonnet:

Fleuve, si le cours de tes eaux
Va rendre l'Ocean prospere,
Si la Fortune moins amere
Après tant de morts et de maux
    Permet aux bienheureux ruisseaux
De l'Espagne, ma douce mère,
Mesler leur onde belle et claire
Avec tes flots, et mes flambeaux:
    Fay une pose pour me prendre,
Et me prens affin de me rendre
A ces bords distillé en pleurs:
    Le feu qui brusle mes moëlles
Pourra, sans noyer ses ardeurs,
Vivre en ses ondes naturelles.

[River, if the flow of your waters goes to make the ocean rich, if Fortune less cruel after so many deaths and ills

Permits the blessed streams of Spain, my sweet mother, to mingle their fair clear flow with your own, and with my flames:

Then stop to take me, and take me away to those shores now trilled by tears:

The fire that blazes within me will burn, without stifling its ardor, amid the ocean's swells.]

His quickness of wit fostered a great friendship with the constable and led to some strange conversations on the subject of religion.

Next came the service that d'Aubigné rendered in the Loro affair that you can read about in chapter 5 of the current book.[10] At about the same time the king of Navarre was disturbed by the great number of men that the lord of Lansac on one hand and the viscount of Aubeterre on the other had gathered in Guyenne on the pretext of a personal quarrel.[11] Lussan, who was in on their game, but seeing no advantage to himself in a bearskin that was being parceled out before the bear had been killed, came alone to see the king. He found him hunting and informed him of the true nature of the affair, which was to take La Rochelle [by slipping in] through the grill gate in front of the mills of Saint Nicholas. D'Aubigné was sent to look into the matter. He went to the city hall of La Rochelle and asked that three men be chosen with whom he could speak in secret. The Rochelais replied that they should all be kept informed because they were all trustworthy. His answer to that was that even Jesus Christ hadn't chosen so well, and he would kiss their hands [in farewell] if they were not willing to comply. So they were forced to select three men for him. They found that all but two of the bars of the grill gate had been filed down; still, he couldn't persuade [the Rochelais] to prepare a trap for the plotters.

A month later those same troops mounted up and moved out. D'Aubigné had promised his master that he would break up any enterprise they had in mind, so he gathered a few guards and some others, ten good men in all, who could be reinforced by the garrison at La Rochelle. And because the others marched by night, he marched along behind them, camping apart by day, and with the plan to [go around them and] rush to the gates of whichever city they meant to attack; and then, with some additional harquebu-siers, he would surprise the attackers [while they were still] a quarter-league away from the city. That is an excellent way to break up an attack.

The king of Navarre, passing through Cadillac, asked the great Candalle, well known by this name, to let him see his splendid study.[12] This was agreed to, provided no disrespect was shown. "No, Uncle," said the king, "I will bring no one less worthy to see it than I." And so in he went, accompanied by the sieurs de Clervaut, du Plessis, Saint-Aldegonde,

Constans, Pellisson, and me. In the meantime, the soldiers waiting outside were having fun with a six-year-old whom they had lift the full weight of a cannon with a machine. Inside, d'Aubigné got ahead of the others and came to a piece of black marble, seven feet square, where the good man kept his notebooks. Finding some brushes and everything else he needed, d'Aubigné took one and, listening to the arguments about weights, wrote:

> Non isthaec, Princeps, Regem tractare doceto:
> Sed docta Regni pondera ferre manu.

[Prince, it is not for a king to learn to lift such things, but to bear with a skillful hand the burdens of his kingdom.]

Having done that he drew the curtain and rejoined the others. When they arrived at the marble, Monsieur de Candalle said proudly to the king, "Here are my notebooks." But when he opened them and saw the distich he cried out twice, "Oh, there is a man here!" The king retorted, "Do you think the rest of us are beasts?" Then he invited his uncle to look at our expressions and pick out the one who had done the trick, which led to much joking and banter, too frivolous to retell here.

The court [of Navarre] came to accompany the queen to Saint-Maixent, where she was to rejoin the court [of France].[13] She had been speaking ill of d'Aubigné since [they had all been together in] Libourne, for she suspected him of a *sfrisata* against Madame de Duras, or at least of having given the idea to Clermont d'Amboise.[14] So with the support of the queen mother she threw herself on her knees before the king her husband and begged that out of love for her he never see d'Aubigné again, to which he agreed. She was furious about his outrageous banter, as in this example:

the maréchale de Retz had given to Entragues a heart of diamonds;[15] when the queen seduced Entragues away from the maréchale, she won the heart of diamonds as well, as a mark of her triumph. D'Aubigné had supported the maréchale against the queen, so the latter would boast to him, "I have the heart of diamonds," but she said it once too often. "Yes," the companion finally answered, "and only ram's blood can cut it."[16]

And so he pretended that he had left the court but in fact spent his nights in the king's chambers, and by this fakery he uncovered his false friends.[17] He took advantage of this time to pursue his courtship, in support of which the king himself wrote letters to his mistress.[18] His rivals and some of her relatives thought that they were counterfeit, so the king came in person and with masques and runs at the ring he honored the quest of his servant. This love affair made the joy of all Poitou with the dancing, jousting, parties, and tournaments that the lover organized, some of which attracted the prince of Condé, the count of La Rochefoucauld, and many other great men. But it also aroused envy, and made many turn against a courtier who, instead of trying to please the rustics, simply dazzled them. Let me tell you one of his many tricks to win her hand.

He instructed his friend Tifardière to say something like this to Bougouin, the girl's guardian, under the pretense of settling their conflict: "You are being pressed by several princes and lords to agree to this marriage with d'Aubigné. I know that your promises and your preferences lie elsewhere. If you agree not to betray me I will show you a way to get rid of him without anyone having reason to complain." After many promises and embraces he continued. "You must assure him that it would be an honor for your ward to marry him, an accomplished and well-bred gentleman. But, as often happens when strangers are involved, his rivals are spreading stories about him that they would not dare maintain in front of him. Ask him to remember how at a party, when certain people had brought charges from Monsieur de Fervacques against him, he said to their faces that if he couldn't change their minds with his denials he would change their cheeks with his fists. He knew that no one would accept the challenge, and that he would have to send his own denials to Fervacques. Since all of this is known to Madame d'Ampierre, the duchess of Retz, Madame d'Estissac, the countess of La Rochefoucauld, and other relatives [of Suzanne] of such rank, he has made sure that they understand that he did not act frivolously [on that occasion]. A deal must be made by which the relatives will agree to sign the marriage contract after they have seen laid out before them his titles of nobility and his genealogy, on the condition, of course, that if he cannot produce them the agreement will end. Because I know very well," said Tifardière, "that he cannot produce such documents."

Bougouin embraced and thanked the messenger, and wasted no time in carrying out the plan. D'Aubigné, who had never cared a whit about wealth, house, or title, had retrieved his family papers along with some furniture from the castle at Archiac, where they had been kept in storage. Being thus assured of his lineage he had laid this trap. To carry it out he chose the sieur de Corniou, a relative of his mistress, to take charge of his papers, and he warned him that if any of the family old enough to fight meddled with them, they would have to answer to him. And so there gathered the sieurs des Marets, de Bougouin, La Taillée, and Corniou, who were able to read the records of a careful investigation that had been made for a lawsuit and quarrel that the sieur d'Aubigné *père* had had with a gentleman named

Ardène when they had fought over their order of precedence in a procession. It showed that he was of the House of Aubigné in Anjou. And because the aforesaid Ardène had encumbered his free holdings and the [fees of the] royal attorneys for the suit it had cost more than one thousand crowns and lasted three years; it was necessary to produce marriage contracts and inheritances for six lines of ascent going back to a Savari d'Aubigné, commander of the castle of Chinon for the king of England.[19] The investigators even inspected a chapel built by him, decorated with the family's coat of arms, which shows the jaws of a silver lion rampant, in armor and langued in gold. The Jousseliniere branch of the family have since furred their lion in ermine. When these facts were revealed, d'Aubigné made these old gentlemen agree to write and sign their assent to the marriage, so that he might know with whom he yet had to deal. Then, on his return from the court of Navarre, and in accordance with the plan, he married his mistress.[20]

FIVE

*

Campaigning for a Kingdom

1583-1589

Three weeks later, back in Pau, [d'Aubigné] finds his master in a wondrous rage over the grievous insults made to his wife in Paris.[1] You can read about the dangerous journey he made to his regret in chapter 3 of the tenth book, in which he did not want to make known his rude resolve to kill right and left in the room if anyone had tried to stab him.[2] Also, [he doesn't tell] that in passing through Poitiers he had his orders copied and certified, and sent the originals for safe-keeping to his wife in a sealed box, with orders not to open it, which she, contrary to the usual behavior of her sex, obeyed. And I should add that Saint-Gelais, then also in Pau, was so worried about his friend's mission that his hair and beard grew beyond all bounds. When the king of Navarre saw his messenger turn into the garden in Pau, the first thing he said to a gentleman who was with him was, "Go tell Saint-Gelais that he can go crop his hair now."

About a year after that the duke of Epernon was working diligently for his own ends to effect a reconciliation of the two kings. The papists close to the king of Navarre con-trived many schemes to get the king to go to the court in Paris, a move which Ségur, head of the Council, opposed

vigorously, and always with the active support of d'Aubigné.[3] So the plotters, who knew Ségur's character, persuaded him to go to court instead. And there he was treated
with such favor that his foolish mind was turned and he
promised to bring back his master. On his return he could
say nothing but that the king was an angel and that the
ministers were devils. He rallied to his support the countess
of Guiche,[4] whom he had been defaming only a little while
before, and the court of Navarre was astounded to see the
king now consider such a journey. Here is the remedy provided by d'Aubigné, who knew Ségur only too well. One
day, as [Ségur] was walking through the hall where the
young men of the court were fencing, d'Aubigné, hot from
his exertions, took him by the hand, led him to a window
that overlooked the rocks of the Baise, and pointing out the
precipitous drop said something like, "I have been asked by
all the good men of this court to show you this drop which
will be for you the day your master leaves for Paris." The
astonished Ségur said, "Now who would dare do that?" "If
I can't do it by myself," replied the other, "there are the
companions who will help me." Ségur turned around and
saw ten or so of the most fearsome, who at that moment
gave a tug to their caps, having been instructed to do so
even though they had no idea of what the conversation was
about. The frightened man went off to see the king, not to
tell of his fear but rather that d'Aubigné was openly calling
the countess of Guiche a witch, accusing her of having poisoned the king's mind, likening her ugly face to the strange
love she had kindled, and that in trying to understand it he
had even consulted Doctor Dortoman about love potions.[5]
And he added that a Huguenot prince had as many overseers
as he had servants, and that what can be acceptable for the
nobles are [judged] sordid pleasures for a king. He also told

the king that Monsieur de Bellievre, when he was lodging across the hall from the countess, saw her go off to mass one day accompanied only by a pimp, a buffoon named Esprit, a negress, a valet, a monkey, and a spaniel. This gentleman, recalling to d'Aubigné the honors shown the lady friends of the king at the royal court [in Paris], asked how it was that the courtiers of Navarre were not as honorable and why this lady went about with so grotesque an entourage. "It is," replied the scold, "because we have in this court a most honorable nobility, but there are no pimps, buffoons, valets, monkeys, or dogs but what you see there."

Soon after, d'Aubigné made a rapid trip into Poitou. On returning he was informed by La Boulaye and Constans that he should turn back, since his death had been promised to the countess and to Ségur. Having received this information in Montlieu he abandoned his gear there, took post horses, and arrived still booted to find, near the quarters of Madame, his friend La Boulaye, who took fright and begged him to get back on his horse. But the other slipped a dagger under his belt, against his usual practice, and following his own plan made his way by secret passages to surprise the king and the countess, who were alone in Madame's private chamber. The king was flustered, uncertain of how to receive him. D'Aubigné, with a proud look and speaking in familiar terms, said to him, "What's the matter, my lord? How can so brave a prince fall prey to such hesitation? I have only come to see if I have done wrong, and if you want to repay my services like a good prince or like a tyrant." The king, all upset, said, "You know that I love you, but I beg you to resolve your quarrel with Ségur." This he went to do forthwith, and surprised Ségur so completely with his rebukes for his heedlessness and the sight of the dagger that the latter went right back to the king to say, "Sire, this fellow is a better man than you or me." And in proof of the reconciliation he paid him 2,500 crowns owed him for his travels and that he never expected to see again.

The queen of Navarre returned to her husband and was reconciled with everyone except d'Aubigné.[6] Still, when he was invited to join in a plot to have her killed, he put an end to the matter with his vigorous objections, for which his master thanked him.

With his marriage he had agreed to buy Le Chaillou, a property in Poitou. The king had been advised by his secretary Parisière that three things should be avoided in that area: the marriage of the prince of Condé because of Taillebourg, that of d'Aubigné because of Mursay, and that of La Personne because of Denant.[7] So he sent out dispatches concerning these matters. But they were done anyway, and the purchase of Le Chaillou was assured by the shame d'Aubigné put on the king's men in Poitiers that in those days such unworthy and base actions were ordered by kings.

Soon after there began the war of the barricades, at the beginning of which the princes of the religion held a notable assembly at Guitres.[8] You have in the eighth chapter of the tenth book a full description of everything that happened there, and in the ninth of the strange and dangerous fight at Saint-Mande. I have nothing to add to it.

Regarding the expedition of the duke of Mercoeur into Poitou I will simply add that d'Aubigné, serving there as executive officer, began to urge that the men on foot be armed with pikes, contrary to the opinion of his master, who hated this weapon. All of that is described under the identity of a *maistre de camp*.[9]

Soon after, Saint-Gelais with fifteen men and d'Aubigné with ten gentlemen forced three companies of foot soldiers to surrender at Brioux. And the capitulation they had them sign included a clause by which they renounced the detestable article issued by the Council of Constance.[10]

The prince of Condé, after having set siege to Brouage, undertook an assault on Angers, with great risks for d'Aubigné, as you find described in the thirteenth and fourteenth chapters of the tenth book.[11] A detail I can tell you is that when Madame d'Aubigné, having heard a rumor that circulated for three weeks that her husband had died in one of the fights that we have described, saw enter her courtyard fifteen horses and seven mules that belonged to him, and his cap and his sword, she collapsed at the sight. What had happened was that when he retreated from one of the suburbs of Angers he sent his gear on with his regiment, keeping for himself only a cap to wear under his helmet, a short sword, and a hauberk. When he finally made his way back to his home he tempered his wife's joy at his coming with two notes that he sent her, one from ten leagues away, for fear that she might die of too sudden a gladness.

Once home he hoped to gain from his misfortunes at least a bit of rest; but the duke of Rohan, the Rochelais, and the ministers in a body urged him in the name of God to regather his regiment and to raise again the ensign of Israel. And they provided him with the means. So he began with the four companies that he had left at the siege [of Brouage] and, having chosen the island of Rochefort as a base, he mustered in all eleven hundred men and marched into Poitou, where he carried out what you can find described at the beginning of tome 3 [i.e., book II, chapter 2].[12] It should be added that he would have fortified himself on the islands of Vas and Saint Philibert but for the urgent requests of the sieur de Laval.[13]

Matters in Saintonge and Poitou being then in a critical state, he decided to seize the island of Oleron, where I must tell about one notable folly of his. When d'Aubigné saw that there was some resistance on the island he instructed his captains that no one should attempt to land before him. Acting on this vanity, he set out in a boat with Monteil de L'Isle and Captain Prou, who did the rowing. They were about three hundred yards from his ship and closing on a fishing boat when they were rudely surprised to see that it was instead a warship under the command of Captain Medelin, a renowned and capable fighter. The latter, with a force of only sixty muskets, but knowing how to maneuver and familiar with the nearby sandbars, hoists his sails and steers straight at the future governor of Oleron. Prou cries out to d'Aubigné, "You are lost. The only way to save yourself is to slip under his bowsprit." No argument about that, so Prou rowed straight at them. Medelin recognized the tactic and had his musketeers take aim and fire straight down on our skiff from twenty yards away. They fired so hastily that Monteil suffered only a few holes in his coat, Prou a slight wound, and the third man nothing. And when they were ten yards beyond the bowsprit, Prou stood up and yelled at them, "Go hang yourselves, you cutthroats, for here is the governor of Oleron." At sight of this our other ships, following behind, fired a volley, but without effect. The men from Brouage then took to their oars and rowed to the sandbar, where they beached their boat. We landed our skiff on the beach, where, with our men close behind, the people of the island took fright and fled. I would like to add to the account in the *Histoire* that on the first appearance [some time later] of the royal naval force of fifty vessels,[14] two launches from Oleron, each with twenty men, rowed out into the middle of the fleet and captured two barks, each of about forty tuns. Despite cannon fire from two galleys the two boats were pulled away from the fleet. One was recovered but the other brought back to Oleron. That's what I can add to the account of the eleventh book, chapter 3.

It should be known, too, that during the whole battle for Oleron d'Aubigné fought in shirtsleeves, except for two occasions when he put on a helmet to scout out an approach. The people of the island had gathered four wagonloads of food, including three dozen pheasants, to celebrate the return of Saint-Luc. But when they approached the town and saw that the fortunes of war had turned, they wanted to slip away, but a good-humored magistrate put a stop to that and brought us the provisions anyway, with this speech: "Monsieur, let us not fool ourselves. It is for the man who will be master here that we have prepared this gift."

The first thing done after the island had been secured was to discharge Captain Bourdeaux, a sergeant-major, because, with orders to defend the most important part of the trenches, he and his men had decided to surrender instead. For that we were going to kill them. But an old captain named La Berte argued that a bloodletting was not good when the fever was high. So d'Aubigné slipped twenty of his gentlemen among the guardsmen to make sure of that company. Bourdeaux's excuse was that his men were mostly papists. After that we began to build a citadel, which was in a state of defense in fifteen days, and in three months it had a double moat, one filled with spring water and the other with water from the sea, and with fish stocked in each.

The king of Navarre, being in La Rochelle, came out to inspect Oleron, but he didn't want to see the soldiers of the island at evening parade because he had been informed by the count of La Rochefoucauld that they were wearing two hundred pairs of scarlet breeches with silver trim that had been taken from the royal seamen. Moreover, the lavish parties that d'Aubigné gave for all the courtiers aroused the envy of the master and of his followers.[15]

Soldiers from Brouage made five landings on the island and they were always beaten, so that there were hardly any left who at one time or another had not been taken prisoner. They were always released on payment of ransom except for those who were taken in the biggest fight and who were used to secure the release from the galleys of Captain Boisseau and his companions. But this happy time came to an end with the capture of the governor, which you will find described at the end of chapter 6, book II.[16] This was followed by his determination to return to prison, whereby d'Aubigné gave a notable example of the value of his word:

Thus he was made a prisoner by Saint-Luc, who assured him of his life provided no instruction was received from the king or the queen to do otherwise with him. The captor and his prisoner became good friends, so much so that he gave him leave to go to La Rochelle on his word of honor that he return to Brouage the following Sunday at five o'clock in the evening unless death or another prison intervened. That Sunday morning Saint-Luc sent word to him that he should not return at the appointed time because ships from Bordeaux, under orders from the king, had come to get him and take him to his death, and with a warning for Saint-Luc of destitution for himself and his family if he failed to surrender his prisoner. The captive would not renege on the pledge he had given with his hand and, when his friends tried to lock him up to nullify the pledge, he left La Rochelle, as if he were already in Brouage, to go to his certain death. When he arrived [in Brouage] he saw the galleys waiting. Saint-Luc received him in tears. But that very night when he was to be put on board, his men captured Guiteaux, the king's lieutenant for the islands, and sent word that he would have the same fortune as their leader. Saint-Luc kept his prisoner, sent away the ships, and rejoiced in secret at this outcome. (*Histoire*, II.6.58–59)

In the extremity of his peril he composed a prayer to God, which the next day, finding himself saved, he turned into an epigram that you can find among his works and that begins: *Non te caeca latent.*[17]

I have mentioned the petty nature of the king of Navarre; here is another example. A young man from a prominent family of La Rochelle, while rebuking a poor soldier who was an aide in the first company, grievously insulted a ranking officer of the guards. For the least of that man's offenses, which was, "I reject your right to command me," the senior officers of Oleron gathered [to try him]. When he admitted that he had twice led the aide into disobedience of orders he was condemned to be shot, a sentence later changed, at the request of the junior officers, to demotion and expulsion from service. But this soldier's aunt, who had procured a cousin for the king's pleasures, reported to him the harshness with which her nephew had been treated. The king seized this opportunity to do ill to his man and sent an official from the council to summon him.

The governor of Oleron, thinking he had been called to give his advice on the approach of the maréchal de Biron,[18] was quite astonished to see the young fellow, well dressed in silks thanks to the earnings of his cousin, and accompanied by the mayor Guiton and twenty other relatives, waiting at the council door. The king appeared in the doorway and made many mocking reverences to d'Aubigné, saying, "God keep you, Sertorius, Manlius, Torquatus, Cato the Elder, and if antiquity has an even sterner captain, God keep him too!" The other, feeling the bite, answered promptly, "If it is a matter of discipline, permit me to reject your authority," which he then did. He went into the other chamber but refused to sit down. He did not mention any of the other charges [brought against the young man] but only his refusal to obey orders. Then he said no more. After counsel was taken Monsieur de Voix, who was presiding, thanked d'Aubigné and encouraged him to continue to defend discipline from the unworthy hands into which it had fallen. Then he added, "We have only one thing to criticize, namely that after having justly condemned to death a man who had rebelled against his duty, you were so bold as to commute the sentence, for this [power] belongs only to the general." D'Aubigné, relieved to be censured only for this, pointed out to the council that being on an island and having the right to cast artillery and to give battle empowered him to give pardons. This was conceded. Then the king was censured at length for his subversion of discipline and good order.

Such harassment, and especially the sale of the island to the enemy, which d'Aubigné could not abide after having won it at such great cost, resulted in his retiring to his home.[19] His grievances, and a just desire for revenge, led him to entertain a wrongful thought that his pains and perils had never before inspired, and this was to take formal leave and to seek his fortunes elsewhere. But knowing that the party was attached to the religion, and he to it as well, he determined—and here is where the devil jumped at his chance—that he would have to stamp out all the effects of his training and upbringing, and study carefully the variations among the churches to see if in the Roman faith there might not be a grain of truth. He was so angry that he couldn't keep his project a secret and it became known, and this made the sieurs de Saint-Luc, de Lansac, d'Alas, and other papist enemies shower him with books. The first that he opened was Panigarola, whom he tossed out as a windbag. The second was Campion, whose elegance he had to admire. But that was not what he was looking for, so when he threw it aside he wrote on the title page *Declamationes* in place of *Rationes*. Next he fell on what we had in those days by Bellarmine.[20] He embraced the method and the strength of argument of his book and admired the evident fairness with which the author presented opposing arguments. He thought he had found what he was seeking. But when he made a careful analysis, with the help of Whitaker and Sidbrand, he ended up more confirmed than ever in his own religion.[21] And he answered those who asked about the fruit of his reading and about his plan that he had ruined it through his efforts because he had been on his knees [praying] from the start. At the end of six months the affairs of the party had sunk to a dreadful low. His master sought him out and, having recently fathered a bastard, wanted to make of the child a gift of reconciliation. D'Aubigné was not impressed by this gesture, but he did come to reconnoiter Talmont.[22]

It was at the time the duke of Joyeuse was preparing his first expedition into Poitou that his Albanians challenged twenty Scottish gentlemen to a private fight, as you will find recorded in chapter 14, book II.[23] I would add here that Rouzilles, godfather to the Albanians, said that if one of the Scotsmen died his Albanians would not wish to reduce their own number from twenty. D'Aubigné replied that in that case he would be a Scotsman. The other then said that [in the same circumstance] he would be an Albanian. D'Aubigné shot back, "Then let's be Scot and Albanian even if no one dies," and on that they shook hands.

His trip and the spirit of the army contributed to the defeat of the two principal divisions of the duke of Joyeuse, as you will see in chapter 15 of book II.[24] As a result of his work and his fighting our man fell into a serious illness that lasted four months. Before he had recovered, on learning of the coming battle, he went to Taillebourg, arriving just after the army had left.[25] For lack of a better escort he picked up fifteen stray harquebusiers, eight horsemen, and a crew of camp followers. Fearing surprise attacks from Saintes he strung them out in as long a line as possible, which was very easy given their lack of discipline, and it served him well because around midnight, along a narrow road in a thick forest, they encountered three companies in three ambushes. With his men strung out he was able to discover the ambushes without his stout fellows getting caught, and to make two counterattacks with enough sword play to chase the rabble away. The soldiers from Saintes carried off one lieutenant and one ensign dead, and some others wounded. On his side there was only one casualty. With these scuffles attended to, d'Aubigné reached the army as it was marching out of Montguion. The next day he served the king as squire as long as he was riding his curtal horses. He was fifth in the deployment of the army, and the king did not reject his advice. He was especially glad to have strengthened the left flank, as you can find in chapter 16.[26] When the main battle began, the king changed horses, and d'Aubigné took a place among the *maréchaux de camp*. After the first attempt [of the enemy] to rally he came upon Monsieur de Vaux, lieutenant of Monsieur de Bellegarde, who seeing him with his vizor raised, which he had done because of the lingering effects of his illness, struck at him with a powerful sword thrust that hit him on his chin piece. Vaux got a thrust through a slit in his helmet that struck him in the eye and pierced his skull. [D'Aubigné] had already met him three or four times in the places indicated [in the *Histoire*]. In the rout of the enemy ten gentlemen of mark rallied to him and begged him to lead them, which he did in three pursuits, where they used their swords and prevented a rally.[27]

The king of Navarre now had a little more elbow room and he decided to carry out a move on Brittany which fifteen years earlier d'Aubigné had proposed be put in the hands of Monsieur de La Noue and later of the viscount of Turenne.[28] The latter fell to his knees to beg the king to give him command of such an enterprise. But this prince, who wished to add nothing to the glory of the one or the power of the other, put off the project for a long time, and then wanted to have it carried out by a more fragile instrument that he could break when it became too bright. So he entrusted the matter to Du Plessis-Mornay and ordered d'Aubigné, as author of the plan and necessary to it, to assist.[29] Because of the great honor, he accepted. But he pointed out to the king that the plan would fail if he subordinated the naval force to the land force when it should be the other way around. And that is how it turned out.

Meanwhile this prince was laying siege to Beauvoir-sur-Mer, where he wanted to make a trench against the advice of his staff. Seeing himself thwarted he turned the task over to d'Aubigné, who, to take the outer defenses, chose eight captains, each with six soldiers. Shielded by hastily made mantelets they began to dig a trench by the edge of the moat. You see something about this in the seventh chapter of book 12.[30]

On their return from there, between Saint-Jean and La Rochelle, the king of Navarre called up beside him Monsieur de Turenne and d'Aubigné and told them of his perplexity about marrying the countess of Guiche, to whom he had made a firm promise. He asked the one and ordered the other to be prepared, when he met them the next day, to give him their opinions, the one as a good friend, the other as a faithful servant. That night Monsieur de Turenne, apprehensive about such a task, found an excuse to ride off to

Marans. The other, bound by his place as squire, resolved to do his duty. The next day, on leaving the city, the king gave strict orders that he was not to be disturbed. Then he took his man and, after a word or two about the viscount's evasion, delivered a two-and-a-half-hour speech in which he reviewed thirty stories of princes, ancient and modern, who prospered when they married for love persons of lower birth. Next he touched upon other marriages in which ambition for a great alliance had turned out ruinously both for the prince and for the state. And he ended up by commenting upon the unfairness of people without passion who try to control an impassioned soul. After all that, he said to d'Aubigné, "And now for this I need your rude sincerity." Then he who had spent the whole night thinking this matter over and who was under orders to speak with frankness began. He first attacked the faithless servants who had researched such stories for the master and who were inexcusable because without passion they had encouraged an excusable infatuation. "These examples, Sire," he continued, "are beautiful and useless for you: the princes you have named were in secure situations, not hounded, not harrassed like you whose soul and status have no other support than your good name. You should consider, Sire, that there are for you four very different conditions: Henry, the king of Navarre, the heir to the throne [of France], the defender of the church.[31] Each of these has its followers whom you must pay in different coin according to their interests. To those who follow Henry you should entrust Henry, that is, the estates of your family. To the servants of the king of Navarre, the offices of your sovereignty. To those who follow the dauphin, pay them with hope, even as hope draws them to you, and tempt them with the promise of your fortune. But payment for those who serve the protector of the church is difficult for a prince, for what they seek is zeal, integrity, good actions. This is the payment you owe to those who are in some respects your servants, in others your companions, but always concerned to shield you from as much danger as they can and to leave to you all honor and profits from your wars. Knowing as I do how you hate to read, I do not suspect you of having found all these bad examples that you have cited by yourself. That was a disloyal labor that should have been left for last by those who took all that trouble to please you by doing you harm. For all those princes named did not have sturdy servants who were both judge and defender of their masters. Their servants had to go to another room when they wanted to vent their complaints and anger. So, Sire, let your thinking be shared here; heed at least halfway those servants by whom you have survived. I have been too much in love myself to think that I can or that I even want to break your heart with my reasoning. You are in the throes of a violent passion. We shouldn't even consider whether or not we can subdue this passion. Rather, to enjoy fully your love, I say that you must make yourself worthy of your mistress. I see by the expression on your face that you find these words strange. Let me explain myself: your love should spur you to carry out your duties virtuously. Accept the advice you now shun, use the best of your time for necessary actions, repress the little private vices that do you harm. And then, when you are victorious over your enemies and your misfortunes, you can follow the example of those other princes because your situation will be like theirs. Monsieur is dead, you have but another step to climb to reach the throne.[32] But accept one more council from my fidelity: do not neglect current affairs for hope in an uncertain future. You have lessened your concern for the state you now have in favor of the one that, God willing, you will have. But, if you lift one leg to mount that last step before it has been cleared—even as it happens when we are fencing—a thrust can knock you flat if it catches you with that foot in the air." The king of Navarre thanked him and promised to keep a two-year truce in his thoughts about the countess.

On arriving in Saint-Jean, d'Aubigné helped his master dismount. Then, learning that Monsieur de Turenne had gone to bed exhausted by the long detour he had taken, d'Aubigné went to tell him about his speech, its end being interrupted by the arrival of the king, who related the same order of arguments given above, but not as coming from the mouth of another but from his own reflections.

The enterprise at Niort was on the docket. D'Aubigné was the last to leave for there, with two servants who were to be sent back to the master, and so he was the first to learn of the death of Monsieur de Guise, which he brought to the companions three leagues away.[33] The assignments he had in the capture of the city were to hold Captain Christophe by the hand, set off the first petard, and then, with the promise of the sieurs de Saint-Gelais and de Parabère to follow, lead the first troop. Unfortunately, he fought with Arambure's men in an action where each side lost three gentlemen and two soldiers, and his good friend lost an eye as well.[34] You have in chapter 15 of book 12 an account of the capture of Niort, and of Maillezais, where d'Aubigné remained as governor to the annoyance of his master, who ordered for him the worst conditions possible to make him give it up. But d'Aubigné was too tired to run.[35]

It was necessary to go to the relief of the garrison of La Garnache, where Monsieur de Chastillon, against d'Aubigné's advice, ordered a retreat by night.[36] Many would have been lost but for the rally led by d'Aubigné. On his return from there he found the king, who had remained sick at La Mothe-Frelon, now in the mood for a bit of fun. He had prepared a false report of a major attack on Maillezais. But its governor had his own people contrive a similar message so he could [have an excuse] to get away from the king. So when the latter message arrived the king said to him, "We planned to give you a false alarm, but here a real one has just come in ordering you to return promptly to your place." This retirement from duty, prepared as a prank, was the first rest, or rather the first break from his labors, that this man had known from the age of fifteen to the thirty-seven or so years that he then had, for he could truthfully say that other than the time lost in sickness or in recovering from wounds, he had not seen four consecutive days without duty.

After the meeting of the kings and the battle of Tours, where d'Aubigné turned up, the king laid siege to Jargeau. There d'Aubigné, indicated as "another with Frontenac" did what you see written in the twenty-first chapter of the same book.[37] He led the *enfants perdus* at the siege of Estampes and was before the walls of Paris with the five mounted scouts whom the king himself led. While still on duty he wanted to challenge Sagonne, so he slipped away to the Pré-aux-Clercs where he called to the nearest horseman, whose name was L'Eronnière, chamberlain of the count of Tonnerre. He was answered with curses and blasphemies, and a challenge to fight, which the other thought impossible [to accept] because of the enormous ditch that lay between them. D'Aubigné, who could see that his man bore silvered arms, decided to look at him more closely, but because of a barleyfield lying between them, he had not seen the ditch. And so he was totally surprised when he suddenly found himself at its edge, so close that like it or not he had to spur his horse forward and gamble all. He was lucky to have a horse that was a good jumper. The other received him on the far side with a pistol shot but immediately felt at his throat the pistol of his foe, who demanded his life or his surrender, even though eight or ten horsemen were riding up to help him. He was taken alive to the prince of Conti and to Monsieur de Chastillon who were no closer than Vaugirard. The king [Henry III], who had just been wounded, took pleasure at the account of this exploit and wanted to see the prisoner, but d'Aubigné, despite his master's order, did not wish (as he said) to play the show-off.[38]

The king of Navarre, now king of France, went to the room of the dying king with eight of his men wearing breastplates under their doublets. Beset as he now was with many responsibilities he closeted himself with La Force and d'Aubigné, who spoke to him as you can find in chapter 23 of book 12.[39]

SIX

✳

Bitter Victory

1590-1610

The first evening that the French and Spanish armies took a look at each other between Chelles and Lagny, the king ordered d'Aubigné to relieve the sentries who had served that day.[1] Some Spanish mounted harquebusiers thought he was a commander and engaged him in a skirmish that he had to join before he could get away. The next day under the king's banner Picheri and he slipped away to warm up a skirmish that they thought was getting too cool. Then they served at Roulet in what you can find at the end of the ninth chapter, book 13. In the same place, you should know that he was the third man with the king and the maréchal de Biron.

In the same book, chapter 11, he carried out the actions ascribed to the *maréchal de camp*, as well as what is told about the captain responsible for the capture of Montreuil.[2]

In the fifteenth chapter it was to him that Ambassador Edmont ran in a rescue attempt, and it was also he whom Arambure saved when he had been knocked off the roadway by two lance blows.[3]

At the siege of Rouen the king honored him by making him a battle sergeant at the appearance of the duke of Parma, and you can see the honor he paid his master at his own and Roger Wilhens's expense.[4] In chapter 22 the speech that follows D'O's is his.[5] To which I must add that in a skirmish before Poitiers he recognized Pluzeau and chided him for riding under the cover of harquebus fire.[6] He was paid for this with a musket shot that struck his horse in the right shoulder and came out by the thigh. This was the same horse, called Passeport, that had jumped the ditch of the Pré-aux-Clercs.

D'Aubigné arrived in Chauny for the siege of La Fère in mourning for his wife, who had died a few months before and for whom he spent the next three years weeping every night.[7] To stop this he would press his side near the spleen; this caused a gathering of blood, which he finally excreted like a lump of lead. What made him go to the siege was that when he participated in a certain assembly that you will see below, his colleagues said that his intransigence was only due to his despair at never being in the good graces of the king and his fear of appearing before him at court.[8] And since the king had sworn before a table full of witnesses to have him killed, he—to change this opinion—made six trips of which this was one. He arrived at the house of the duchess of Beaufort, where the king was expected.[9] Two gentlemen of mark urged him most warmly to get back on his horse because the king was in such a fury over him. And indeed he overheard some other gentlemen arguing whether he would be turned over to a captain of the guards or to the provost of the household. In the evening he sat down among the torchbearers who were waiting for the king. When the royal carriage appeared in front of the house he heard the voice of the king call out, "There is my Lord Sir d'Aubigné." Although this seigneurial greeting was not to his liking he still went forth to meet the king. The latter presented his cheek, ordered him to help his mistress, and had her remove her mask to greet him. He was also heard to say to the companions, "Is the provost here?" The king, having ordered that no one was to follow, then led d'Aubigné along with his mistress and her sister Juliette into his private quarters. For more than two hours he had him walk back and forth between the duchess and himself. And there were said the words that have since become so famous. When the king in the torchlight showed him his cut lip,[10] he endured and did not take offense at this reply: "Sire, until now you have only denied God with your lips. He is content with piercing them. But when you deny Him in your heart, He will pierce you in the heart." The duchess cried out: "Oh, such eloquent words, but ill used." "Yes, madame," said the other, "because they will serve for nothing."

With this lady so boldly in love, and seeking the friendship of our author, the king wished to establish her and to make plans for the care and education of his little Caesar, today the duke of Vendôme.[11] He had him brought in naked and laid in the arms of d'Aubigné, who was to take him, when he was three, to Saintonge and there raise him among the Huguenots. But, since this plan went to the winds, we will send the telling of it there, too.

More useful will it be to add to the end of the thirteenth chapter [book 14] that the king, struck down by a serious illness, summoned d'Aubigné, who was about to leave, and kept him for two hours in his chamber. After kneeling twice and praying to God [the king] ordered him, in the name of all the harsh but honest truths that he formerly bore upon his lips, to tell him if he had sinned against the Holy Spirit.[12] D'Aubigné, after trying to get a minister to take his place, began by speaking about the four marks of such a sin: first, awareness of the sin when committing it; second, inviting with one hand the spirit of error while with the other rejecting the spirit of truth; third, lack of repentance, which cannot be real if there is not total hatred both of the sin and of oneself for committing it; the fourth and last was loss of hope in the mercy of God. The king was then advised to examine his own conscience to decide the matter. After a discussion of four hours and six prayer sessions, the dialogue was broken off. The next day the king felt better and wished to hear no more of it.

You have heard that the anger of the king was aroused because of the affairs of the religion. Know, then, that a few months before, at a synod at Saint-Maixent, d'Aubigné at a round-table supper began to revive some of the matters that had long been neglected.[13] You can find the results of this in chapters 11 and 12 of the book we are running through.

After that, at the great assembly that lasted almost two years, meeting successively at Vendôme, Saumur, Loudun, and Châtellerault, d'Aubigné was always among the three or four to confront the king's deputies on the floor, where he made several statements that poisoned the mind of his master against him and even more the opinion of the court.[14] President Canaye, formerly Le Fresne, attended when he had already made up his mind to abjure. The duke of Bouillon, formerly the viscount of Turenne, admitted him among the leaders and, wishing to win more glory than the other men of note who were negotiating at Châtellerault, then spoke out strongly in favor of royal power over that of the party. At this d'Aubigné, who observed that the next six speakers had lowered their tone mightily, raised his own higher than usual when he took the floor. Le Fresne-Canaye rose up in the middle of his speech and cried out, "Is this how you treat your duty to the king?" The speaker turned to him, saying, "Who are you to tell us about duty to the king? A duty we embraced before you were even a schoolboy? Do you want to make your own fortune by setting duty to the king against duty to God? Learn not to interrupt, but to keep silent when it is necessary." They became very incensed. And when Le Fresne cried out: "What are we coming to?" the other replied, "Ubi mures ferrum rodunt" ["Where mice gnaw iron," a classical periphrasis for a never-never land]. This struck the minds of the assembly as appropriate, it being at the time on the topic of security places.

The ill-respected president in turn represented the affairs of d'Aubigné badly with the king. And the duke of Bouillon insisted that he should show more reverence for such a magistrate. "Yes," said d'Aubigné, "to one who is going to renege," which he did within three months.[15] Finally, all the bitterness and hard feelings of the assembly were blamed on d'Aubigné, and for that he was called *le bouc du désert* because everyone discharged his hatred on him.[16]

The king's anger with him did not matter, however, when the case of Cardinal Bourbon was on the docket. He had been declared king by the League and was already appearing on coins in France as Charles X.[17] The king was advised that he should not be taken from Monsieur de Chavigny at Chinon and put under d'Aubigné's guard at Maillezais, and Monsieur du Plessis-Mornay supported this by recalling d'Aubigné's rancor and constant quarreling with the master. But the king replied that d'Aubigné's word, properly given, was sufficient proof against all that.

This cardinal-king becoming then his prisoner, the duchess of Retz[18] sent to the governor an Italian gentleman, who, having secured a safe-conduct when he was still two leagues from Maillezais, delivered this letter:

Mon Cousin, I beg you to accept by this bearer the assurance that we send you, Monsieur le Maréchal and I, of the perfect friendship and cordial concern that we have for your advancement and for the welfare of our cousins your children. You may show by your actions that you are sensitive to the wrongs done you by looking kindly upon the opportunity by which I hope to prove myself your very etc. etc.

The Italian then exposed his mission, which was to offer 200,000 ducats cash, or the governorship of Belle Isle with 150,000 crowns, in return for looking the other way when the prisoner escaped. The reply, not put into writing, was that "the second offer would be much more satisfactory for I might then eat the bread of my treachery in peace and security. But, because my conscience follows me so closely that it would join me in the boat when I sailed to the island, go back where you came from, and take comfort in my assurance that without my promise [of safe conduct] I would send you to the king."

There was in Poitiers a Captain Daufin who was brigandizing the marshes of Poitou and Saintonge. Having been ill-treated by the count of Brissac as a result of a quarrel, he sought revenge at the very time that the Leaguers were making all kinds of attempts to save their king, who was a prisoner at Maillezais. When Daufin made known to d'Aubigné that he wished to speak with him in secret, there came two warnings from Poitiers and one from La Rochelle that this Daufin was in the hire of the count of Brissac to kill d'Aubigné. The latter, having made his own plans to catch the count, [ignored the warning] and took steps to ascertain Daufin's intentions. Having arranged a meeting with him at dawn in an abandoned house, the governor set out from his stronghold alone, had the drawbridge raised after him, and, finding his man, addressed him as follows: "I have been warned not to talk to you because they say you have been hired to kill me. But I didn't want to miss this chance to talk with you. Let's clear up this suspicion by an honorable means. Here is a dagger that I brought so that you might have the choice of your blade or mine to carry out your promise. So if you want to try, you can do so, and with honor. And there is a boat I brought so that you can save yourself through the marshes." Daufin on hearing this speech threw down his sword at d'Aubigné's feet and made as honest a submission as a brute can make, and thus they entered into each other's confidence. Take note of this story as one of my great follies.

Some time later Du Plessis-Mornay had his meeting with the bishop of Evreux.[19] D'Aubigné arrived in Paris two weeks later, and the king had him engage in a similar debate that lasted five hours in the presence of four hundred persons of mark. The bishop managed to elude his adversary's arguments with his great powers of reasoning, so the latter developed his own demonstration, the two premises for which he took from the bishop's own reasoning. This knot so belabored the mind of the bishop that there fell from his brow onto a Chrysostom manuscript enough perspiration to fill the shell of a medium egg. The debate came to an end with this syllogism:

> Whoever is in error in a particular matter
> cannot judge of that matter;
> The Fathers are in error in the matter of
> controversies, as is apparent in the fact
> that they contradicted one another;
> Therefore, the Fathers cannot judge in the
> matter of controversies.

The bishop approved the form and the major premise,

but the minor remained to be proved. [For this] d'Aubigné
wrote his treatise *De dissidis Patrum*, which the bishop never
answered, even though the king pledged that he would.[20]

You have at the end of the thirteenth chapter of [book 15]
a notable speech ascribed to a governor who was considered
a violent partisan. That's d'Aubigné, who showed thereby
how his violent attachment to the affairs of the Reformationists still did not let him stoop to unjust actions.[21]

Soon after, the duke of La Trémouille, object of the king's
hatred, died;[22] and d'Aubigné, seeing no one left on whom
he might call for help in case of oppression because of the
corruption and subventions that were eroding the party, had
a coastal vessel made ready at Esnandes to which he sent
four of his trunks. And as he was loading the last two a
courier arrived from the king with letters, some written in
the king's own hand, and others from the duke of Bouillon,
at that time with His Majesty, and from the sieur de La
Varenne, all confirming his welcome at the court. The letters
of this last, the least worthy, gave him most reassurance,
although the king had written in his own hand with the
familiarity of the old days, of which his children have many
examples, as a sign of unusual cordiality. Thus summoned,
he spent two months at court on the pretext of teaching La
Broue and Bonouvriers how to organize jousts and tournaments.[23] During all this time the king never said a word
about the past. But one day when the first squire of the king,
Liancourt, had the squire on duty yield his place to the dean
of squires, the latter accepted and, on entering the lists, was
addressed by the king as follows: "I haven't yet spoken to
you of your assemblies where you almost ruined everything
because you were good while I was managing to corrupt
your most important people. I even made one man my spy
and your traitor for six hundred crowns. How many times I

said to myself when I saw that you were not following my wishes:

> O que si ma gent
> Eust ma vois ouie!
> Et puis, j'eusse en moins de rien
> Peu vaincre et deffaire et caet.

> [Oh if my followers
> My voice but heard,
> Then, so quickly done,
> I could have bested, overrun, etc.]

But what can I say, you poor fellows, there were but a few of you working for the affairs of the church, and all the rest were working for their purses, and to earn my good will at your expense. I can boast that a man from one of the best families of France only cost me five hundred crowns."

After more of such talk d'Aubigné replied thus: "Sire, I fell into my election. I tried to flee it when others were practicing it. The oath I took was forced from me. I can't forget it, nor can I explain it. I only know that all our most notable brothers, except for Monsieur de La Trémouille, were selling their labors to Your Majesty since they were there to serve his interests. But I would lie if I said the same. I was working for the church of God, with all the more dedication as it was oppressed and weakened, for we had lost you as our protector. May God in His mercy not cease to be yours. Sire, I would far rather abandon your kingdom, and life itself, than win your good graces by betraying my brothers and my companions." The king's response was strange. "Do you know President Jeannin?"[24] When I said no he continued, "He was the brains of the League. He spoke to me in the same terms as you. I want you to know him, because I have more trust in you and in him than in all those who played a double role."

To this exchange I would like to add another that took place when I left the court. After a strong embrace d'Aubigné turned back to the king and said, "Sire, seeing your face I am emboldened to ask my master that which a friend asks of a friend. Undo three buttons at your breast and tell me how you could have hated me." The king turned pale as he always did when he spoke with emotion, and he said, "You loved La Trémouille too much." The reply: "Sire, that friendship was made in your service." Question: "Yes, but when I turned against him you did not cease loving him." Reply: "Sire, I was brought up at the feet of Your Majesty when it was beset by so many enemies and misfortunes that it had need of servitors who were devoted to the afflicted, who would not forsake their duties, but who would redouble their loyalty even as your enemies' strength grew. Please be patient with that apprenticeship in virtue." There were no more words, but simply an embrace *à Dieu*.

It would be well, since we have spoken of Monsieur de La Trémouille, whose probity you can judge in the *Histoire*, [chapter 1, book 15], to tell you how those who held firm for the party were in constant danger of death and had taken an oath to die, if need be, together. When the king sent some troops to surround the duke at Thouars, the latter wrote to d'Aubigné: "My friend, I invite you according to our oath to come die with your very faithful. . . ." The answer was: "*Monsieur*, your letter will be properly obeyed, although I must reproach you for one thing, namely to have evoked a promise which I have too constantly in mind for it ever to be recalled." The two of them went riding about the country one day to rally their friends when they came upon a village where the day before a few heads had been taken and some assassins stretched on the wheel. D'Aubigné, noting that the duke changed color a bit on seeing that display, took him by the hand and said, "Take a good look because, with what we are about, we must harden ourselves to death."

Two years later there took place an assembly at Châtellerault to which the duke of Sully was sent.[25] Monsieur de La Noue and d'Aubigné were elected in absentia to represent Saint-Maixent. That was why the latter, on his arrival in Châtellerault, begged to be excused from this unexpected election, because the ill-feeling he would arouse would disserve matters entrusted to him. Then he went out while [the delegates] deliberated. But instead of acceding to his request they ignored his excuses and charged him to go to the duke of Sully (who claimed the right to preside) and tell him to stay away from the assembly except for the occasions when he was to speak for the king.

At the end of the assembly the duke of Sully, after ordering him in the name of the king to leave, was himself obliged to leave for reasons much too complicated to describe here. The duke had confided to the delegates the authorization for strongholds which he had earlier denied having, and which he disavowed after having shown it.[26] In the same session the assembly spent three days trying to straighten out the problem of Orange. It was so entangled that the interests of the king, of the prince of Orange, of the churches of Dauphiné and Languedoc, of the maréchal de Lesdiguières, of the city of Orange itself, of the sieur de Morges, the sieur de Blaccons, and other notable lords all collided.[27] When they saw no way to unravel the knot someone proposed that one man alone be entrusted with drawing up a solution which would be easier to amend in writing than in speech, where words fly off in the air. D'Aubigné, chosen for the task, asked for three days to work on it. He then left the assembly, took some paper, and with his memory still fresh sketched out a plan. When he reflected that if he spent any more time on the plan it would be no less gone over and marked up, he returned to the assembly, where he was reproached for not going to work on his assignment. He simply placed his paper on the table [and left the room]. Recalled in half an hour, he found after a scolding that they had changed one syllable only. He has ever since that time thought that this was the most fortunate of his writings.

Three years before the death of the king,[28] d'Aubigné went to Paris and stayed with Monsieur du Moulin, where he met Messieurs Chamier and Durant and four other pastors to the number of seven. They told him that he had arrived at a time when their ears were ringing with talk about the reconciliation of religions. There was more discussion of it than ever, which to them was a sure sign that some new double dealers had been bought. They agreed with their visitor on a few points which he proposed to them to put an end to this fraudulent propaganda. He asked them in particular if they would support him in a daring proposal that he had been considering. His plan was to restrict all the controversies about the church to the rules that could be found to have been firmly established in the early church by the end of the fourth century and the beginning of the fifth.

Chamier moved to support him and was followed by the others. D'Aubigné then makes his appearance at the court and finds the king in his privy chamber, who, before anything else, told him to go see Du Perron. This he did. The cardinal received his guest warmly and with unusual kissing on the cheeks. The two were no sooner seated than the cardinal made a great show of weeping over the misfortunes of Christendom and asked if it were not possible to do some good. Response: "No, for we are not good." Question: "Monsieur, oblige Christendom by taking some initiative to put an end to so many pernicious controversies that divide the minds of individuals and of families, as well as of the kingdom and state." Answer: "Monsieur, initiatives are useless when the last thing you name tries to control the minds of our leaders."

After several such starts d'Aubigné, who had restrained himself, made this proposition: "Since you want me to go beyond my competence and my condition, it seems to me, Monsieur, that the advice of Guicciardini should be followed in the church as well as in the state. He said that properly constituted things which fall into decay may be corrected by restoring them to their original form. I shall therefore make a proposal which you, who always like to fall back on origins as if they were to your advantage, cannot refuse. I propose that you and we accept as inviolable laws the constitutions of the church as they were established and observed until the end of the fourth century. In everything we agree is corrupted, you—who call yourself the eldest— can begin by restoring the first thing we ask of you; we will do the same for the second, and so on, until all has been restored to the forms of the early church." The cardinal exclaimed that the ministers would never hear of such a proposition, to which the other replied that he would pledge his head and his honor that it would be respected. The cardinal, now pensive, pressed his hand and said, "Give us forty years beyond the four hundred." Response: "You need more than fifty, for I see that it is the Council of Chalcedoine that you want.[29] Receive us in public debate, and when the main premise has been conceded we will give you what you want, but there and not here." Question: "Please, tell me what you would ask of us first, for you would not dare yield to our first request, the placing of crosses which was done without question within the time period you have set." Response: "We would hold them in the same honor that they did then for the sake of peace. But you would not dare—I won't say grant—even discuss our first request, which would be to restore the authority of the pope to what it was during the first four centuries. For that we would even throw two hundred more years into our bargain." The cardinal, who had been poisoned in Rome and who came back angry, exclaimed that we would have to do that in Paris since we could [never touch it] in Rome.

The discussion was adjourned for another time and d'Aubigné returned to the privy chamber, stopping briefly on his way to speak with President Langlois. On his arrival the king asked him if he had seen his friend and what they had talked about. As he reported on the talk, there in the chamber, which was full of important people, the king let slip, "Why did you say to Monsieur le Cardinal, on his request for the Council of Chalcedoine, that you would concede it in public debate and not then and there?" The answer was, "If after conceding four hundred years the doctors still wanted fifty more, that would be a clear admission that the first four hundred years were not enough for them." A few cardinals and Jesuits who were in the chamber began to grumble out loud, and the count of Soissons, to whom they had been whispering, said quite clearly that such pernicious talk should not be tolerated. The king knew he was offending them, and he was also embarrassed for having let it be known that the cardinal had revealed his private conversation with d'Aubigné before the latter had even arrived. He turned his back and went into the queen's chamber.[30]

Some days later the king, being advised to arrest or silence a man who had ruined the project for reconciliation —for afterward there was no more talk of it—said to the duke of Sully that they would have to put this troublemaker in the Bastille and that they could surely find something to charge him with. One evening Madame de Chastillon sent for him that she might tell him something.[31] On his assurance not to betray her she begged him to leave the city or he was surely lost. D'Aubigné, after replying that he would do what God counseled, went off to pray and did not take her advice. Instead, early the next morning, he goes to see the king, makes a little speech about his past services, and asks for a pension, something that he had never done before. The king, delighted finally to find something mercenary in his soul, embraces him and grants the request. The next day the companion went to the Arsenal, where the duke of Sully greeted him and and took him to visit the Bastille, assuring him that there was no longer any danger for him, but as of one day only. The following Sunday on leaving divine service Madame de Chastillon, amazed to see so strange an outcome, invited to dinner Monsieur du Moulin, d'Aubigné, and Mademoiselle de Ruvigny, wife of the man in charge of the Bastille. This lady, touched by a comment she heard at table, fixed her eyes on the second of the two men and began to cry. Pressed to tell the reason for her tears, she said that she had twice prepared a room for him, the second time expecting the victim at midnight.

In short order the king completely changed his views and took d'Aubigné so warmly back into his good graces that he thought of sending him to Germany as ambassador general and having the individual agents there report directly to him twice a year on their activities. But then this project was changed when the king conceived of a greater one, which he communicated to him despite d'Aubigné's objection that such information should be given only to those who would bear responsibility for its execution.[32] Nevertheless, since he was at the time vice-admiral of Saintonge and Poitou, he did not wish to remain idle amid such great activity. He urged the king to launch a part of his plan against Spain herself so that, while rapping the knuckles of his enemy elsewhere, he might also send an arrow into her heart. And when the king rejected the idea, invoking the old saying, "Who goes weak into Spain is beaten, who goes strong starves to death," d'Aubigné proposed a deal which, for a million in gold, would provide for two fleets to sail along the coasts of Spain carrying supplies for the armies at the going prices of Paris. He brought Des Escures into his scheme, but it was stopped when the duke of Sully adamantly opposed it.

So, taking leave to return to his work in Saintonge, he heard these words from the king: "D'Aubigné, do not be deceived. I hold my life, temporal and spiritual, in the hands of the Holy Father, the true vicar of God." On that he left, feeling that not only was the great plan for naught but also the life of that poor prince condemned by God. And thus he spoke to his closest friends. Two months later came the frightful news of his death. He heard it when he was in bed. The first report was that [the king] had been struck in the throat, but he said to several who had rushed to his room with the messenger that it was not in the throat but in the heart, for he was sure that he had not been wrong.[33]

*

SEVEN

Early Retirement

1610-1620

[After the assassination of Henry] the queen was now declared regent by consent of the provincial assemblies, with no one objecting in the assembly at Poitiers except d'Aubigné, who insisted that such election was not in the power of the Parlement of Paris but of the states.[1] And although he was reported for having voiced this opinion he was nevertheless [among those] sent by his province when it made its submission [to the queen].

In Paris [Protestant] deputies from different places waited until nine provinces were represented, and then they made plans together to have themselves presented [to the queen and her son] by the sieur de Villarnould, deputy general at the time.[2] There was a lively dispute about their manner of entering and how they were to speak, and they finally agreed to ask d'Aubigné as the oldest and most experienced to serve them as a guide. The royal council was scandalized that not one delegate knelt either at the beginning or at the end of the speech that the trembling Rivet insisted on delivering, and which he did in an awkward manner. As they filed out Monsieur de Villeroy scolded d'Aubigné and asked why he had not bent his knee. The answer was that the group was made up of nobles and clergy only, who owed the king reverence but not on their knees.

Four months later the queen took it into her head to speak in private to d'Aubigné.[3] With the note he received from her, and against the advice of his friends, he went by post [to court] and remained closeted for two hours with the queen, the door being guarded by the duchess of Mercure. She pretended that she had wanted to consult with him on a matter of importance, but in fact it was to make him unfaithful, or suspect, to his party.

So now we are at the assembly of Saumur,[4] at the opening of which Monsieur de Boissise made great promises to d'Aubigné, getting only as a reply: "I shall have from the queen just what I want, namely that she consider me a good Christian and a good Frenchman." Afterward they sent La Varenne to him to court him in the most extravagant manner, so much so that when one of the corrupted delegates said to him one day in the presence of Monsieur de Bouillon, "What has La Varenne been doing going to your house so often, twelve times since yesterday morning?" the answer was, "What he did at your place on his first visit and has yet to do at mine after twelve."

It was there that he lost the friendship of Monsieur de Bouillon, which he had held for thirty years on all occasions.[5] This happened when he prevented him from presiding [over the assembly] and opposed him in all the curious proposals which cost him his reputation, especially the one by which the lord duke tried to persuade the party to renounce its guarantees and to place itself entirely under the protection of the queen and her council. In support of this he delivered a long and emotional eulogy of the time of our martyrs, after which he heard a totally different speech, which ended like this: "Yes, martyrdom cannot be praised enough; blessed beyond measure is he who endures it for Christ; to prepare for martyrdom is the sign of the true Christian. But, to be responsible for it, or to entice others into it, this is the sign of a traitor and a murderer." At the end of the assembly d'Aubigné, who was thought never to say *à Dieu* but to those who were going to revolt or to die, said *à Dieu* to Ferrier before the whole group. This was received most bitterly by Ferrier and several others until his revolt, which happened two months later.

After that the affairs of the religion and of the party as a whole began to decline, first among most of the gentry, and then with the ministers because of their greed. Among three of the unfaithful, Ferrier and Recent were punished with shame, but Rivet, discovered in Poitou to be receiving a pension in the name of his son, was hated by few among his fellows, and was admired by the young ones. He was compared to the dog who stuck his head into a jar of butter and then the little dogs came to lick his muzzle in congratulations. Thus, at the synodal assembly at Thouars, which met to report on Saumur, the *fermes* were often the butt of derision. There in the midst of two hundred persons assembled we actually saw the minister from Parabelle named La Forcade rise to his feet eight or ten times to interrupt the speakers: "Messieurs, we must take care not to offend the queen." When we wanted to check up on the governors who were cashing in on their garrisons, some young ministers said, "They are simply being prudent and peaceful." When we wanted to do something about those who were accepting pensions to the detriment of the party, another minister said: "Principibus placuisse viris non ultima laus est" ["To please princes is no small praise"—Horace, *Epistles*, 1.17.35]. With this new kind of farce d'Aubigné took leave of the company, alleging his age and saying that he had had enough of public assemblies, for they had now become like public women.

The duke of Rohan, hated and out of favor for having served the party well at Saumur, retired to Saint-Jean, seemingly to fortify himself with friends.[6] d'Aubigné, whose garrison like the one at Saint-Jean was not being paid any more, seven thousand francs of pension having been taken away for his refusal to accept an increment of five thousand, was obliged to go find his pay on the Sèvre River.[7] In those days he was afraid of being besieged, so he scouted the site of Le Dognon because he was determined not to be the *sorice d'un pertuso*.[8] He bought the little island and began to build a house in Maillé for two thousand crowns. Parabère was ordered to inspect the construction; d'Aubigné was there and gave him dinner.

The following year Parabère was again ordered to look over the cow barns under construction at Le Dognon, and he told the builder to be present for his visit. The other replied that it wasn't worth the trip and that the inspector was simply looking for a meal. This sarcasm convinced the inspector of the unimportance of the construction and that it amounted to nothing. But then one morning there arrived on the scene thirty masons, fifty workers, some canvas tents, three guns, and stores. That raised an alarm in his camp and sent him scurrying and dashing off messages. But he got no response.

The duke of Rohan scarcely had to be summoned to the first uprising of the prince of Condé and of the duke of Bouillon, and he gathered his friends at Saint-Jean.[9] D'Aubigné, unable to give up his own project, was asked to lend his support to the prince and his followers. For an answer he sent them just two lines: "We are willing to shoulder the burden of your war; spare us that of your peace."

That first uprising faded away with an agreement and an
amnesty for everybody except d'Aubigné, whose only recourse was to fortify his two places and make the second
ready for attack. And after various plottings and dealings
that year we saw the prince of Condé's war break out.[10] He
chose d'Aubigné to be his adjutant and sent him dispatches,
but the latter did not want to receive his commission from
[the prince's] hands but rather from the [delegates of the]
churches who were meeting in Nîmes.

The duke of Sully, governor of Poitou, went to Poitiers,
where he assured the queen with the backing of twelve leaders of the province that it would not stir for the prince of
Condé. Then he came with promises and threats to Maillezais to secure the same agreement, adding that all the leaders
of Poitou would keep their word. He got as a reply that he
had forgotten one leader, who would give his decision the
next day. By this was meant the first drumbeat of the regiment that [d'Aubigné] had raised for his son and which, the
next day, took to the field. That very day the sieur d'Ade
with the garrison from Maillezais took Moureille by petard.[11] Within two weeks the duke of Sully had organized
his own forces. It happened that four companies from our
regiment and one company of the duke supported by light
cavalry arrived at the same time at Vouillé to make camp.
Our infantry chased his cavalry as was proper.

Monsieur de Soubise mustered his forces and marched to
join the prince of Condé with seven regiments amounting
to more than five thousand men.[12] One morning the duke
of Bouillon, marching to the siege of Lusignan, met d'Aubigné heading for the same task as adjutant. There they
settled their differences of Saumur. But after that there was
nothing to this war worth writing about except that toward
the end d'Aubigné, against the wishes of the prince of

Condé, managed to lay siege to Tonnay-Charente, where he got half his body burned in an accident and had to be carried back to the trenches. But the whole campaign led to nothing more than the treaty of Loudun, which turned out to be a public market of general cowardice and individual treacheries.

The prince of Condé, who in council called d'Aubigné his father and who had bankrupted him as if he were doing him honor, called out from a window as he saw him leave, "*A Dieu en Dognon.*" The reply was, *A Dieu à la Bastille.*"[13] When the prince arrived at court he repaid him for his good services, including the mobilization of five thousand men; expenses of sixteen thousand crowns duly acknowledged, counted, and unpaid; and his salutary advice, which he had ample time to ponder while he was in prison. He repaid all this by reporting in secret council that d'Aubigné was an enemy of the throne and capable of preventing any king from ruling with absolute power as long as he was alive.

This same prince persuaded the duke of Epernon to read *Les Tragiques*. And, after pointing out to him the barbs in the second book as if they were aimed at him, got him to swear the death of the author, as indeed was attempted there and elsewhere, and in various ways.[14]

This duke then came to bully La Rochelle.[15] The Rochelais begged d'Aubigné to come to their assistance, and they had him call and then dismiss his troops no less than three times, so uncertain were their negotiations with the enemy. The latter moved up at a time when there were no more than 150 men left at Maillezais. And then it was learned that the [duke's] troops from Saintonge had arrived and were in Mauzé. When d'Aubigné found this out, as well as that one of his regiments had been sent on patrol, he was sick at heart that one of his parishes was left open to pillage, for until then he had spared it from the ravages of war. Because of the drought that year it was no longer an island, and he saw that a hundred wagons abreast could have crossed the marshes [that surrounded it]. He hastened, therefore, to make a show of the forces that he had. To put a good face on a bad game, when he saw six companies of cavalry arrive at Cour-çon, he left the peasants of the region armed and in view on a rise of land. Then he and his 150 men marched out at two o'clock in the afternoon to make camp at Morvins in the face of the enemy. He ordered his men to march in file and, as soon as they got there, to run around behind the village and join the end of the line. Thus, Reaux, adjutant in com-mand of the advancing troops, sent word to the duke advis-ing him that he faced at least 800 men. This information brought up four more companies to reinforce him. Still, d'Aubigné had noted their fright and he chased them out of a house where they had come foraging and indeed made plans to seize it himself the next night. But as he was about to set out for that, he received word from the duke that an agreement had been reached with the Rochelais.

The two gentlemen who brought him this information boldly invited themselves to dinner at Le Dognon, where they began to speak freely of the hatred of the duke for their host. They reported that he had said aloud before five hun-dred gentlemen that if he couldn't have it otherwise he would challenge him to come to a field and to see one of the finest swords in France. The reply to all that was, "I was not so poorly reared that I am unaware of the rights of dukes and peers, or of what we owe them, or of the privilege they have not to fight [with the likes of me]. I know even better the respect I owe to the colonel-general of France, under whom I have the honor to command infantry. Now if an excess of anger or valor has moved Monsieur d'Epernon to command me absolutely to see this fine sword in a field, certainly he will be obeyed. On another occasion he showed me one, on the guard of which there were diamonds worth twenty thousand crowns. If it pleases him to bring that one, I will consider it an even finer sword." One of the gentlemen replied that Monsieur le Duc had qualities that he could not cast off for a test of courage. The answer: "Monsieur, we are in France, where princes born in the cover of their greatness would be skinned if they took it off. But note: one can still strip off one's furnishings and acquisitions. The duke has nothing in that respect to make him unequal to me." Then the older of the two gentlemen said, "Well, Monsieur, even if all these matters were settled, there are still many lords and gentlemen with the duke who would prevent him from assuring you of the privacy of a field in which to fight." D'Aubigné, now aroused, could not keep from saying that he would take care of that problem and could assure him of a field in the very jurisdiction of the duke which he himself would secure from his foe's friends. And with that the conversation ended. When it was reported to the duke it made him again swear vengeance, spiced with insults.

For a long time d'Aubigné had made a nuisance of himself with the advice and warnings that he sent to those who were in positions of responsibility, and there wasn't an assembly with which he did not share the wisdom of his long experience. But he had also once seen a master plan of what was to happen, which he had got from the hands of Gaspard Baronius, a nephew of the cardinal, and the one who was called to a knowledge of God for having condemned to death the little Capuchin in Rome.[16] Well, this fellow had managed, thanks to his uncle and to his own talents, to become a member of the congregation of what is called the *Propagazione della Fede,*[17] and he was chosen to be one of the three agents that this council sends each year to the three corners of Europe with memoranda on the whole of Christendom. On his trip to Spain, well provided with gold and authentic dispatches, he sought asylum in Briançon with Monsieur de Lesdiguières, who had him taken by one of his men to Paris, where he was introduced to a group meeting in the house of Monsieur de Bouillon. D'Aubigné and Monsieur de Feugre were chosen by the group to interrogate Signor Gaspard. He laid before them memoranda for all of Christendom, organized by provinces, and showed for each province two registers, on one of which was written *Artes pacis* and on the other *Artes belli*. The two interrogators then asked to see the papers on the province that was in the most imminent danger; the man showed them first *Rhetorum commentarios*, since persecutions were to begin there before the general crusade was launched.[18] That is how d'Aubigné acquired his reputation for making predictions, and made himself importunate as well, and not for having in his house the mute, for which he was criticized. Still, that was such a remarkable thing that I should at this point tell you about him.

He was a man (if one can say man, for the wisest thought him a devil incarnate) who looked to be about nineteen or twenty years old, deaf and dumb, horrible eyes, livid face. He had invented an alphabet of signs and finger motions by which he could express himself marvelously. He had been four or five years in Poitou, staying first at La Chevrelière and then at Les Ouches, striking awe in everyone with his ability to divine anything that was put to him, and helping to recover lost property in the region. Sometimes as many as thirty people were brought to him, and he would tell each one his genealogy, the trades of the great-great-grandfathers, great-grandfathers, and grandfathers, how many marriages for each, how many children, and then all the money, coin by coin, that each one had in his purse. But that was nothing compared with his knowledge of things to come and of the most secret thoughts, with which he would make everyone blush or turn pale. Our honorable theologians (whose censure is to be feared in matters like this) should know that it was the most esteemed ministers of the region who brought this strange man to d'Aubigné's attention. When he settled him in his house he ordered his children and servants, under pain of punishment, not to inquire of the mute about the future, but as *nitimur in vetitum* ["We strive for the forbidden"—Ovid, *Amores*, 3.4.17] that was all they asked him.

It would take another book to tell you everything that man knew about the great men of France and the words that they were exchanging at the very moment he was being questioned. We took care to inform ourselves closely about the court for a whole month, the hours of the king's walks, [the persons] who spoke to him in the course of the day. And when this information was compared with the mute's answers a hundred leagues distant, he was never wrong. The girls of the house asked how long the king would live, and how he would die. He specified for them three and one-half years, as well as the carriage, the city, the street, and the three knife blows to the heart. And he told them everything that King Louis is doing today as well as the sea battles around La Rochelle, its siege, the dismantling of its walls, the downfall of the party, and many other things that you can find in the *Epîtres familières*, which will be printed.[19] And you can confirm with others who were brought up in the house with you the truth of these things.

The enemies of d'Aubigné, to discredit his warnings, said that he got them from the mute, and by this allegation made his salutary advice useless. Well, the truth is that he was scrupulous never to ask of that medium a single thing about the future. Rather, it was his long service and experience that gave him the wisdom to predict those things which have since come to pass.

At the two assemblies held at La Rochelle he tried to ensure that his charges and strongholds be turned over to trusted persons, and thus kept from the duke of Epernon and the bishop of Maillezais, who were dealing with him through intermediaries.[20] A part of the assembly readily agreed to his plan, but the government of La Rochelle opposed both him and the syndics of the people, who supported him. So it chose Maître Bardoni to look into his demands, and this corrupted lawyer concluded that Le Dognon and Maillezais should be demolished if possible. So a month later Monsieur de Villeroy wrote to d'Aubigné at Maillezais in these terms:[21] "What would you say of your friends, for whom you have sacrificed eight thousand francs in revenue, refused an increase of five thousand more, lost the good will of the king and your own pains so many times? They are asking us most insistently to tear your house down over your ears. I haven't changed a word of your friends' terms. If it were up to you to reply to them, what would your answer be? I await your advice."

The answer was, "Monsieur, if it is your pleasure that I be your clerk in drafting a reply to the request of the Rochelais, it would be as follows: Let it be done as requested at the expense of whoever wishes it." When Monsieur de Villeroy reported these lines to the Royal Council, President Jeannin said with an oath that he understood them well. "It means," he said, "that he fears neither us nor them."[22]

Such language, along with measures taken for the defense of the forts, resulted in Vignolles, a marshal in the royal army, being ordered to find out what sustained d'Aubigné's boldness. He came to see him as a friend and as his mentor in the king's household.[23] He reported back two things, the strategic importance and the strength of Le Dognon. In support of the first he added that La Rochelle, the siege of which was being considered at that time, could not be invested unless the valley of the Sèvre, commanded by d'Aubigné's two forts and capable of feeding two-thirds of Spain, was made secure to supply bread for the royal army. The army would pay dearly for its bread if the supplies had to pass through the corridor between Surgères and Mauzé at the mercy of these forts, for nothing would get through that wasn't escorted or lost. And he added a bit more to make his point. As for the strength of the places, he reported that Maillezais would require a full-scale siege and that it would be harder to invest Le Dognon than to take La Rochelle. That's why they next sent agents to deal with him.

Monsieur de Montelon was the first entrusted with the task [of buying the properties] and, when he couldn't manage it, La Vacherie. It would be amusing to recount all the ruses by which these negotiations were prolonged for about two years, after which the duke of Epernon, represented by the marquis of Brèse, offered him as much as 200,000 francs in cash. But instead, d'Aubigné turned his places over to Monsieur de Rohan for 100,000 francs, half in cash, the balance to be paid later. Then he retired to Saint-Jean-d'Angély, where, once settled, he completed the printing of his *Histoire* at his own expense. He considered it a great honor to see it condemned and burned before the Collège Royal in Paris.[24]

EIGHT

✳

"No Separate Peace"

1620-1630

It was at this time that the little war of the queen mother began.[1] Monsieur de Rohan summoned the governor of Saint-Jean, d'Aubigné, and eight of his friends to Saint-Maixent, as if to seek their advice on whether or not he should involve himself in the war. But the proposition he laid on the table was not that at all. He asked d'Aubigné in particular about the preparations and provisions necessary for an army of sixty thousand men to lay siege to Paris. D'Aubigné replied that he had had the honor twice before to be invited to the preparations for that very siege, and that he remembered more or less how one had to go about it. But instead of speaking to this unexpected proposal he begged the duke to consider the confusion that would follow and that would lead to the weakening of their great party once he got involved. And to provide him with a way out, as well as to make himself obnoxious, he asserted that he would not bear arms for the party, nor would he again take his little sword down from the wall.

But on taking leave of the duke he said to the two brothers, "I have assured you that I will not be of the queen's party, but I will join the duke if need be, and you will find me very useful." That being said he returned to Saint-Jean, where [he found that] the rebellious elements of the city, having learned how the besiegers of Paris had been whipped at Ponts-de-Cé, had risen up in revolt and chased out the authority of the duke, his lieutenant, and his captains.[2]

The duke wrote his friend to remind him of his promise of help in case of need. D'Aubigné found the [Rohan] brothers and La Noue with two regiments, amounting to 1,500 or 1,600 men, and some 100 horsemen in all. They had no place to retreat to, except Saint-Maixent, and no base where they could have held out two days. They were drifting toward Bas-Poitou when he took the wanderers in hand and pointed them at an action that he had planned in advance. But that very evening came news of the truce made between the queen mother and those of his own party who were willing to accept it.[3]

After that the king lost no time filling Poitou with his troops, and d'Aubigné resolved to come seek a shelter for his old age and death in Geneva.[4] The followers of the favorite [Luynes] were looking for him everywhere and had sent orders to the principal cities and especially the river crossings for his arrest. So he set out with twelve well-armed horsemen and, making good use of his knowledge of the roads, managed on the first night to slip through three regiments and three guard companies from the army. Along his escape route he had some timely bits of luck, as when a regiment of soldiers blocked his way in the suburbs of Châteauroux. There a peasant whom he met by chance got him across the river at an unguarded place. He had similar luck when his group was separated by a guide they had chanced upon as they were passing through an unfamiliar part of

Bourges. He approached some gentlemen and ministers for help, and they, without knowing him but impelled by a sense of his need, served him as guides themselves.

When the pastor of Saint-Leonard was taking him to Conforgien, he made a detour to show him the miracle of a woman seventy years old whose daughter had died in childbirth. The old woman pressed the new-born infant to her breast and cried out: "O Lord, who will nurse this little one?" At these words the baby grasped one of the grandmother's nipples and instantly her breasts filled with milk, with which she had been nursing the child for eighteen months. Before this story was made public it was first confirmed by public declaration of the church.

At Conforgien the lord of the place hired a man called Petit Roy to guide his guest. That night this worthy arranged with a few gentlemen of the area to prepare an ambush. But the next morning Petit Roy, after speaking to d'Aubigné, felt uneasy. No longer willing to serve as guide he found another man—who took a different route. This story was confessed by one of those gentlemen as he lay dying to his mother, who had raised him in the religion.

In Mâcon he sent his escort through the city in pairs. An old man in the center of the city stopped one of his men and whispered in his ear, "You are smart to go through like this, two by two." From there Monsieur Fossiat sent him on to Monsieur d'Anières, who took him to Geneva.[5] But first, there had been an uprising at Gex, and as a result he ran a great risk carrying arms, for they had been banned in that area. Some from the garrison promptly nabbed a few members of his escort, and would have arrested him, too, but for his stout resistance. He was lucky to get away without killing anybody. Otherwise he would have been captured and lost, because if his flight had been even slightly delayed the marquis of Cypières, the king's lieutenant who was in close pursuit with his portrait in hand would have [caught him] and taken him back to France.

He finally arrived in Geneva on Thursday, the first of September 1620, where he was received with more courtesy and honor than a refugee could expect. In addition to the ordinary courtesies which all notable foreigners receive in this city, he was visited in his lodgings by the first syndic, who took him to holy services and seated him in the place of the first syndic of the preceding year, a place usually reserved for princes and royal ambassadors. They arranged a public banquet for him to which the whole seigniory and a number of foreigners were invited. At the banquet they served some very big marzipans that displayed the coat of arms of the newcomer. After he had stayed for some time with the sieurs de Pelissari and de Tournes, the house of Monsieur Sarrasin, which has since been bought by the princesses of Portugal, was rented for him by the city [and he lived there] until he was able to acquire his own house by marriage.[6] They showed him their military stores and revealed to him their secrets. And when he asked to inspect their war bands, sixteen in number, this was granted, although such a thing had not been done in twenty years. They formed a war council consisting of seven men only, in which he was given full authority. The arrangement lasted until the council was asked to take an oath of loyalty and secrecy. When d'Aubigné learned that his colleagues were obliged to report their important business to the Petty Council, he consented to take the oath of loyalty, but not the oath of secrecy unless his fellows were exempted from revealing what they judged should be kept secret from everybody. When the troops from Savoy were withdrawn, the council ceased functioning because of these difficulties.[7]

During that time the whole city was employed in building the fortifications that he had the honor to plan in both the Saint-Victor and the Saint-Jean sectors.[8]

He had not been in Geneva six weeks when the general assembly of La Rochelle sent by two separate routings an extraordinary testimony to their regret in having so wrongfully treated him.[9] They sent him, first by way of Paris and then by the sieur d'Avias, one of their deputies, their authorization to commit all that the churches in general and the Rochelois in particular could provide for the needs that will be explained below. They also sent him offical letters for the four Protestant cantons, the city of Geneva, the Hanseatic cities in general, all the Protestant princes—twenty such letters with the name of the addressee left blank and the seal open in the manner newly adopted by the aforesaid assembly—and even more letters for members of the churches and specified ministers, all for the purpose of assuring the authority of their representative.

Next there came instructions for him to persuade the Swiss to provide a free levy of troops and to allow the passage of any other troops that he could raise. And along with that a commission [for him] to command the army thus formed. There were four copies in parchment of each of these documents, two sent by each of the routings, except for the letters, of which there were only single copies.

When the sieur d'Avias arrived at Saint-Julien, dressed like a peasant, he sent his messenger ahead in similar disguise to arrange for a place to meet, for he was well aware of the fear of France which made the Genevans cautious. He was lodged in one of the huts recently built for the fortifications project, and it was there that a response to the assembly was drafted. D'Aubigné had asked the Twenty-Five to select two men to whom he could confide secret information, but when these two wanted to report everything to the whole group he was obliged to restrain them with the help of the other two.[10]

At that time Monsieur Sarrasin received word from Count Mansfeld who, having been soundly beaten in Bohemia, was seeking a new master to serve.[11] When his overture was repeated d'Aubigné began to negotiate with him as well as with the two dukes of Weimar. After several missions back and forth at considerable cost to the purse of the representative, the three were engaged to lead 12,000 foot soldiers, 6,000 cavalry, 12 pieces of artillery, half a battery, pontoons, and requisite transport to the river Saône. There they would be joined by three regiments of 2,000 men each that d'Aubigné would raise. For his part he would then serve as adjutant general as long as these forces were together. Everything would proceed on the credit of the assembly until the army reached Forez, where the troops would receive two payments, which would really be half of the whole, since, by the terms of the agreement, they were to receive only half their pay until a peace had been won. Then they would be paid in full from funds guaranteed by the salt works at Aigues-Mortes and Peccais, still presumed to be in the possession of the party.

All these details had been settled and Mansfeld had already advanced as far as Alsace when d'Aubigné, waiting for 200,000 pounds in credits from La Rochelle, was informed that some helpful soul in La Rochelle had suggested that the whole enterprise would be better managed by Monsieur le duc de Bouillon, and the suggestion was blithely adopted. The count therefore turned toward Sedan, and there followed what you can read in the *Histoire*.[12] And the representative was left in the lurch with five hundred pistoles of expenses. His children will take care to keep the documents concerning this affair.

During these negotiations the authorities at Berne sent the son of their first magistrate to invite d'Aubigné to come visit them. That was at the time that Frankenthal was under siege. He accepted, and was received most lavishly with banquets, cannonades, and other honors so extravagant that he had to chide them for it. This first trip led to a second, which lasted some three to four months.

After inspecting Berne he proposed, against the advice of all the other great captains who had visited it, that the city be fortified. That was contrary to the wishes of the principal members of the people's council and to their laws and oath, but he felt that it had to be. The duke of Bouillon wrote to him, as well as to the principal councillors, and stressed the unfavorable nature of the site [for fortifications] and the fact that the city was in the heart of the country. In reply he was told that the site on the contrary was advantageous for fortifications, and that the heart is only a finger removed from the ribs.[13]

The people of the city were so hostile to the very word "fortification" and so keen for the word "battle" that on one of his first tours of inspection a few drunkards carrying halberds approached him shouting that they should throw the Frenchmen who had come to violate their customs into the Aar. In the face of this kind of opposition the consultant, supported by Graffenried, Erlac, and a few other citizens, tried to enlist the support of the ministers. [At their request] the head minister accompanied the seigniory to look at the construction site. Moved by some impulse he asked them all to give thanks to God then and there for this salutary enterprise, after which he knelt down to pray. The members of the seigniory and the crowd that had followed did the same thing, and thus they found themselves committed to the undertaking. The next day almost the whole population came out to the site. After a minister had made a great harangue, a psalm was sung, a prayer was said, and then d'Aubigné brought up his stakes. With a deep bow he presented one to Monsieur Manuel, first magistrate, who in turn wanted to give the honor of the first act to the planner. The latter refused. So we had to hold a council to settle these courtesies. Finally, urged by all to drive the first stake, he accepted the honor, threw his hat to the ground, knelt to pray, then shouted as he struck the first blow with the maul: "May this be to the glory of God, to the preservation of His church, and to the defeat of the enemies of the confederated Swiss!" Then the first magistrate and all the lords pounded on stakes to mark the walls that none in Europe can now surpass in natural advantage. On the pretense of coming to see the project, the Bernese made a show of the strength of all their districts, estimated to number as many as forty-eight thousand men.

Afterward a tour was made of all the cities of the canton, and the military camps, seven in number with one in reserve, were inspected. In a council meeting Monsieur de Graffenried put a pen into d'Aubigné's hand that he might sign the oath of a captain-general, but he refused on the excuse that he didn't know the language. So then he was asked to recommend someone else for the position. He suggested they choose from among three men, namely the vidame of Chartres, the sieur de Montbrun, and the count of La Suze. They picked the last.

The seigniory of Basel sought to be advised from the same hand and sent the sieur de Lutzelman for the arrangements. But of the twenty-two bastions planned for them by the sieur de La Fosse they contented themselves with four and left the city in the imperfection in which it remains to-day.[14]

During the time of these travels Ambassador Squaramel contacted him on behalf of the Most Serene Seigniory [of Venice] for the purpose of naming him commander of the Frenchmen to be enlisted in their service. Everything was coming to a favorable conclusion when Miron, ambassador of the king of France in Switzerland, wrote to the Venetian ambassador that the Republic would incur the anger of the king if it employed a man who was so hated by his majesty. His friends argued to no avail that what aroused the hatred of kings should in fact find favor in republics: fear prevailed over their desire to enlist his loyal service.[15]

Having broken up this affair Miron next tried to have d'Aubigné expelled from Geneva. He tried four different means. The first was to complain that he was spreading libels throughout the city. The remedy for this was to request an immediate investigation. The second attack was to make public a letter [of complaint] from the king which identified the man without naming him.[16] This time the Seigniory, with help from the accused, wrote the following reply [to Miron] about the affairs of the city:

As to the rest of your letter concerning certain parties settled in this city, convicted of and condemned for terrible crimes, as well as of having made agreements and taken actions inimical to the respect due to the majesty of the king, we can assure you, in regard to these two points, that never has any person come to lodge a complaint in this city (as you know has occurred several times) who has not received proper justice, as prompt and severe as he would have received in the place where the [cause of] action might have taken place. When it pleases those who want to file a complaint to send an agent here authorized to bring charges and in possession of evidence to support such charges, specifically, with orders from your king and your own warrant, we will endeavor to cooperate in the name of that reputation for justice which our predecessors have established. In regard to anything that concerns the king directly we will apply ourselves with all the vigor and all the rigor necessary to show in what esteem we hold so precious a reputation. We made this evident last year when a gentleman who had settled in this city filed a complaint about a report which had been made by you similar to the one you cite on this occasion. Two lords of the council, former syndics, were immediately delegated to make a careful investigation, leading either to the acquittal or to the condemnation of the accused. Their investigation lasted six months, during which time the gentleman was confined within the walls of the city.

While these things were going on d'Aubigné bought and fortified the property of Le Crest, which in the end cost him eleven thousand crowns.[17] It should be noted that when he was up on the fifth floor he broke a scaffold when he jumped on it. With one hand he managed to grasp a stone, no bigger than a fist, which had just been set. That hand, with two wounds in it, held the weight of his whole body and gave him the opportunity to consider two sharply pointed posts waiting below to impale him if the help of his people had been delayed. God did not wish to leave him out of danger at any time or place.

The persistent attempts of the court [to make him move] convinced him that he should leave so as not to prove an embarrassment to the city to which he had vowed his life, but the constant threats [of war] and the likelihood of a siege held him there. Thus he made use of Le Crest to stay out of but not far from the city, as his friends had advised.

The third attack on him was a rude one, for without being summoned, much less heard, he was sentenced to have his head cut off for having built bastions from the stones of a church that had been damaged in 1562.[18] This was the fourth death sentence for such crimes which have turned to his honor and gratification. But it was also a means to discredit him in Geneva and to block a marriage which he had begun to plan.

The marriage was with the widow of Monsieur Balbani of the House of Burlamachi in Lucca.[19] It was initiated by the good will of the people, who could wish no more for a woman so greatly loved, as much for her probity, charity, and good works for all, as for her noble lineage, her property, and her wealth. The day before the marriage contract was to be signed the condemned man thought as follows to himself: "If I am dealing with an ordinary mind and heart, with a person who is not ready to risk her life for the cause that threatens mine, she will be frightened and break off the marriage when she learns of this sentence. But if I have met a soul above the ordinary, a soul prepared to join another which has resolved never to surrender, this will let me know it, and will make me very happy." Having resolved this, he brought the news [of his death sentence] to her, and this was her reply: "I am very happy to share God's quarrel with you; what God has joined together man will never put asunder." And so the marriage was celebrated the twenty-fourth of April 1623. Monsieur Foissia offered this quatrain for the occasion:

> Paris te dresse un vain tombeau,
> Genève, un certain hymenée:
> A Paris, tu meurs en tableau[20]
> Ici, vis au sein de Renée.
>
> [Paris has raised a false gravestone,
> Geneva bids you marry today;

In Paris you die in their fancy,
Here live in the arms of Renée.]

Shortly before his marriage he dismissed with proper remuneration the four gentlemen who had stayed with him until then, and settled down to a more simple household with his wife. He turned back to the seigniory the honors and perquisites of their mansion, happy that he was no longer the object of talk for having the place of honor in the church, for which some German princes had been grumbling. The seigniory still gave him a most comfortable place in the church where he had formerly seen a Palatine prince and several great French captains.

It is time now to recount that when he inspected the fortifications of Saint-Victor he found that two bastions had been splendidly situated by Monsieur de Béthune but hastily and cheaply built. He wanted to make them stronger, and did so with the materials that can still be seen there. And, because they extended too far from the ramparts, he designed a new wall to connect them. He did not, however, wish to carry out the new construction unless it became necessary, not only because it could be done later, even within view of an enemy, but also because he wanted to spare the owner of the land and avoid the animosities that often arise from such confiscation. But the owner, who was powerful in the city, being the son of one of the best syndics that Geneva had had and who was himself procurator-general, was too outspoken in defense of his interests for the taste of the seigniory.[21] They issued an immediate order, with instructions to their engineer to mark out the connecting wall within two hours or face dismissal. The seigniory then moved to put the workers to the task immediately. D'Aubigné tried to postpone things, but his request and reasons were overridden by their firm resolve. Thus he ended up with the hostility of a family so powerful that when one of them had a lawsuit before the tribunal of the Two Hundred, sixty of the magistrates had to be disqualified because they were related to the litigant.

Their hostility grew and found a variety of ways to vent itself. For example, when the *Histoire universelle* was being reprinted they said it would arouse outrage in France.[22] And when the old marquis of Baden first found refuge in Geneva they spread the rumor that he had come at the instigation of d'Aubigné to raise an army and that this would provoke the emperor.[23] But it was shown that there had never been any contact between the two men in person or in writing. The accusation simply made evident the ill will of several who were subsequently shamed by it when they saw the marquis live quietly in Geneva for five years, with the exception of a trip to Denmark.

They played a number of other mean tricks against him, like persuading the people that this foreigner had advised the lords to restrict their liberties, that he suggested new burdens for them, and other such things which were all proved to be false, and they called him a man who had been chased out of France because he was a republican.

But their last scheme really inflamed his enemies and even took his cooler friends by surprise. This came about when Rozet, deputized to the court of France with Monsieur Sarrasin, manipulated the secretary of state Herbaud so skillfully with his letters and one that he got [Sarrasin] to write that—at the time that the loss of La Rochelle, the defeats in Languedoc, and the disasters in Germany were frightening the faint-hearted—the lord of Le Crest was confined to his house for three months.[24] And they were not spent without danger, for at that very time someone—who might have been the duke of Epernon or the bishop of Bordeaux, or perhaps the two together—dispatched as many as ten assassins to kill him. For two years they made a great commotion in the country, rejecting their salvation (about which they had precious little to say) if they didn't kill him. But the man they were stalking took his precautions and in fact sought out his killers. He wrote to Monsieur de Candale and urged him to advise his father that he should hire better workers.[25] In the end nothing was decided in Geneva that would have banished him, because the better minds prevailed in the end and because he enjoyed the friendship of the people.

Sometime earlier the lord constable, about to embark on his campaign against Genoa, sent the councillor of state Bullion to d'Aubigné, despite the fact that at their last meeting in Saumur they had become enemies. This was for the project in Franche-Comté.[26] To carry it out three old regiments were to be given to the poor *desterrado*, and for [Bullion] a new one with a company of gendarmes. But it all smacked of the same dithering that was to mark that whole war.[27]

Soon afterward the count of Carlisle, ambassador extraordinary and [his brother] the chevalier, returning from Constantinople, passed through Geneva.[28] They paid deep honor to d'Aubigné and invited him most warmly to come to England. He was taken with the idea and even reserved a place on the boat that the count was having prepared in Strasbourg for his return.

But he was kept from this project for the same reason which on two earlier occasions had held him back. This was the strong evidence that there was to be a siege of Geneva, which that year was ill-supplied with all things at once. But this name England, and what transpired between him and the count of Carlisle, obliges me to recount things which I would rather have left unsaid.

As God does not wish that His graces cleave to flesh or blood . . . Constant, first and only son of d'Aubigné, was raised by his father with all the care and expense that one could have lavished on a prince. He was educated by the finest tutors of France, brought from the best houses at double pay. But the wastrel was corrupted in Sedan with drinking and gaming, abandoned his studies, and finally ruined himself gambling in Holland.[29] Shortly after, in the absence of his father, he married a wretched woman in La Rochelle whom he later killed.[30] The father, wanting to keep him away from the court, gave him command of a regiment that he had raised at his own expense for the prince of Condé's war. But nothing could satisfy the insolence of that lost soul. He rushed to the court, where he lost in gambling twenty times more than he could repay. And for that he could find no remedy but to renounce his religion. He was welcomed as a sublime spirit far superior to all others of the time. When his father learned of his familiarity with the Jesuits he forebade him such company. [The son] replied that in fact he had taken up with Fathers Arnoux and Du May.[31] The old man replied that these two names formed αρνον-μαι [arnou-mai = I renege]. But he carried on, until he finally received from the pope a brief that permitted him to attend sermons and communion services of the so-called reformed religion. After that he returned to Poitou to take over the forts of his father, who, the better to keep him out of trouble, gave him the lieutenancy of Maillezais and made him responsible for its entire administration when he retired to Le Dognon. Maillezais soon became a gambling den, a bordello, a counterfeiters' workshop. And the rascal soon boasted to the court that there were no soldiers left who weren't loyal to him rather than to the father. The latter, informed of these developments by the churches of the re-

gion and especially by a lady of the court, put some petards
and a couple of ladders in a boat and made his way to the
rear of Maillezais. He went on alone, in disguise, to get to
the gate of the citadel. When a sentinel tried to stop him he
jumped at his throat, dagger in hand, and disarmed him.
Then he chased out everyone he thought was disloyal. The
wicked son, thus dislodged, retreated to Niort to the protection of the baron of Navailles, a renegade like himself. And
there he began to plan an attack on Le Dognon, which by
then had been sold to Monsieur de Rohan and was under
the command of the sieur de Hautefontaine, who had a lieutenant who was very faithful but useless in a fight.

One afternoon the governor of Maillezais, confined to
bed with a fever, received a report from a renegade captain
who was in the service of his son, but who nonetheless felt
an obligation of gratitude to the father, that the son was
proceeding with fourscore men by boat and another troop
by land to capture either Maillezais or Le Dognon that
night. The sick man called for his breeches, summoned
thirty-six men from his garrison, which at that time had no
lieutenant or sergeant, and mounted a pony, determined to
go lie in wait for his son at a point on the road which he
would have to pass for either enterprise. He had gone a half-
league with his fever rising when his son-in-law Monsieur
d'Ade and two other men rode up. Monsieur d'Ade threw
himself to his knees and pleaded vigorously that he should
return to bed. When he won the argument he took command from the father and continued on. Two hours later he
found his brother-in-law marching with twice as many men
to capture Le Dognon. But he attacked them anyway and
took sixteen prisoners, whom he turned over to Monsieur
de Rohan, governor of the province at the time. The latter
never managed to bring them to justice.[32]

Constant, to whom the king had said that he would be a father to him now that he had lost his own, soon found himself held in contempt by his people, and in horror and scorn by those he served, rejected by everyone except La Brosse, a notorious bawd, and the whores who supported him. He made overtures to his father for a reconciliation. The reply was that when peace had been made with the heavenly father the earthly one would follow. He came to Geneva, presented himself before the ministers, made there, in Poitou, and in Paris all the confessions enjoined upon him, wrote furiously in verse and in prose against the papacy, obtained money, and finally a pension such as his father could provide from his own funds.[33]

He was advised to go see the king of Sweden with assurance that he would get a commission soon after his arrival.[34] But this was too far away for his ambitions, so he changed his route and went to England. Note that the father was so suspicious of his treachery that the son could not get him to write letters for him to the king of England or to the duke of Buckingham, but only to a few friends, and these with reservations.

So he went to England and explained his lack of letters as due to the dangers of the roads. This was at a time when the king of England, concerned about the situation in La Rochelle and considering war, called a meeting with the duke of Buckingham, four milords, the sieur de Saint-Blancard, who had been sent by Monsieur de Rohan, and this wretch, [dealing with him] as if he were the representative of his father. They decided on war and on the first steps to be taken. One was to send for d'Aubigné. The mission [to summon him] was given to the chevalier Vernon, but the wily one, because he was the son, took it away from him.[35]

So he returned to Geneva and made his report to his father. He was asked repeatedly if he had not passed through Paris, for [not to do so] was the most specific clause in the pact of friendship sworn by the son to his father. The latter knew full well that the wretch's mind would not be his own in that bordello. He denied it with all kinds of oaths. Nevertheless he was made to describe his trip, and in the telling his father became suspicious of certain details and as a result decided not to make the journey to England. So he dismissed his son, entrusting to him useful general information, but not the specific things that he wanted. The son sensed this lack of trust, complained of it, but got no more.

But on his way from Geneva he had in fact passed through Paris and had seen Monsieur de Schomberg by night. And on his return trip he saw both him and the king, again by night, and, grateful for so signal an honor, told them everything about the affairs of England. That is what destroyed the love of father for son.[36]

The old man, to protect his name from the vile actions of his son, thought seriously about going to England, and accepted the offer of the count of Carlisle's boat. But the war in Mantua had lined the frontiers of France, Italy, and Germany with armies in a year when Geneva suffered a shortage of wheat, salt, and other necessities and could not have endured a month of siege.[37] Her enemies were well informed of these facts. And so, although he had made himself obnoxious for five years by his begging and badgering to remedy these weaknesses, judged that there was no separate peace for him. He could do no less than resolve to drop all his other concerns and to await in Geneva an honorable death.[38]

APPENDIX A

*

The Rival Clans

Here briefly is a sketch of the great noble families and of their more prominent members who competed for place and power in sixteenth-century France.

LORRAINE

The House of Lorraine, with its claim of descent from Charlemagne, included among its princely families the ambitious Guise, raised to ducal rank by Francis I. The first duke, Claude, was father to three famous children: Marie, who married James V of Scotland and was mother to another Marie (1542–1587), who became queen of France as the young bride of Francis II and queen of Scotland until ordered killed by Elizabeth; Francis (1519–1563), the second duke, a warrior to whom military victories and an aggressive stand against Spain brought great credit. He came into real power during the brief reign of Francis II, his nephew by marriage, but then he fell from favor under Charles IX and the regency of Catherine de Médicis. Still, as the self-proclaimed champion of Catholicism against the rising challenge of Protestantism, he continued to play a strong role until he was killed by an assassin at the siege of Orleans in the first war of religion; Charles, Cardinal de Lorraine (1525–1574), prelate and diplomat, whose cunning and intelligence matched his brother's prowess and prestige.

Duke Francis's children carried on in the next generation: Henry (1550–1588), the third duke, rode the tide of resurgent Catholicism as leader of the League, plotted with Spain, and openly challenged his king, Henry III, until he was murdered at Blois; Catherine (1552–1596), a conspirator against the throne like her brother, was thought to have instigated the assassination of Henry III; Charles, duke of Mayenne (1554–1611), succeeded Henry as leader of the League until he finally yielded to Henry IV.

MONTMORENCY

The House of Montmorency was led in this period by Anne (1493–1567), whose services to Francis I were rewarded with the governorship of Languedoc and, after 1537, the office of constable. But his ineptitude and his willingness to deal with Charles V led to a fall from favor. He rebounded under Henry II, only to find himself pressed by the duke of Guise. When the latter came into real power with Francis II, he again found himself eclipsed. But when Francis II died he made common cause with Guise and Saint-André (as the Triumvirate) to stem the rise of Protestant influence around young Charles IX. He was killed in battle at Saint-Denis in the second war of religion. His sons, Francis (1530–1579) and Henry, count of Damville (1534–1614), became leaders of the religiously neutral faction called the *politiques*. Equally illustrious were Montmorency's nephews in the Coligny branch: Odet, cardinal de Châtillon (1517–1572), who converted to Protestantism; and Gaspard, admiral de Coligny (1519–

1572), another convert who became one of the great leaders of the Protestant party until he was killed in the opening action of the Saint Bartholomew massacre.

BOURBON

The House of Bourbon traced its ancestry back to Saint Louis and thus claimed its share of royal blood. But its glory was tarnished in the sixteenth century by the treason of Charles de Bourbon against his king. At his death (in the service of the Emperor Charles V at the siege of Rome in 1527) his cousin Charles, duke of Vendôme, became head of the family. His children included: Antoine (1518–1562), who married Jeanne d'Albret, and thus became king of Navarre and father of the future Henry IV, and flirted with Protestantism before rallying to the throne to serve in the first war of religion, in which he was killed; Charles, cardinal de Bourbon (1523–1590), memorable mostly because he was elected king of France as Charles X by the League after the assassination of Henry III; and Louis, the first prince of Condé (1530–1569), who, shunned by the court for his uncle's treason, turned to Protestantism to the point of proclaiming himself the protector of the reformed churches. Louis was virtually banished under Francis II, when he was thought to have plotted the Conspiracy of Amboise, but he returned with such influence under young Charles IX that he pushed the erstwhile rivals Montmorency and Guise into their alliance and sparked the beginning of the first war of religion. He was killed at the battle of Jarnac in the third war. Louis's son, Henry I de Bourbon, second prince of Condé (1552–1588), shared leadership of the Huguenot party with Henry of Navarre. The namesake in the next generation, Henry II de Bourbon (1588–1646), was born under an unfortunate cloud, his mother, the high-spirited Charlotte-Catherine de La Trémouille, being suspected of both adultery and murder. He was raised a Catholic, but this did not inhibit him from joining the Huguenots in uprisings against the regency of Marie de Médicis. If Henry IV had not remarried and fathered the son who would be Louis XIII, this Condé would have been king.

A Religious Conversion?

D'Aubigné often referred to a spiritual change or conversion (e.g., see the end of chapter 1 and chapter 6, above), but it is difficult to reconcile the references for specificity. I am persuaded after careful study of the relevant texts that if there were an authentic conversion it occurred in the late autumn or early winter of 1572 at Talcy while he was in the coma resulting from the wounds he received from an unknown assailant at the entrance to an inn in the Beauce (chapter 2). An autobiographical poem, which his editors have entitled *Elégie*, written in 1578 or 1579, includes a description of this experience in convincing detail but without indicating the circumstances. In the poem he tells, after first recounting the misfortunes of his childhood and youth, how he came of age in the wars:

> Parmy des gens de pied cinq ou six ans entiers
> J'apprins des enragez les dangereux mestiers
> Et à n'avoir discours que de jeuz, de querelles,
> De bourdeaux, de putains, verolles, maquerelles,
> Renier Dieu de grace et braver de bel aer,
> Mespriser tout le monde, arrogamment parler. . . .

Mais quand les fausses Paix chargerent nos miseres,
Mes desseins contentoient mes espritz temeraires,
Car j'estois Capitaine et parfait dessus tous
Aux vices adorés et du temps et de nous.
Dieu estoit mort pour moy et son yre alumée,
A ce point foudroya sa main severe armée,
Me frappa insolent, changeant de furieux
Sur un lit, en deux jours, le sens, l'âme et les yeux:
Je trouvay Dieu encor' et par la maladie
Qui me mit à la mort je retrouvay ma vie.

[For five or six whole years among the foot soldiers I learned their dangerous crafts, to have truck only with gambling, with fights, brothels, whores, the pox, and bawds, to blaspheme and to put on a bold air, to despise everybody, to speak with pride. . .

But when the false peace burdened our miseries, my projects satisfied my foolhardy spirits, for I was a captain and accomplished beyond all in the vices adored by the times and by us. God was dead for me and His wrath enflamed; at that point His stern hand cast a fiery bolt, struck me down, insolent, and changed from my fury, on a bed, in two days, my sense, soul, and sight; I found God again and by the pain that left me at death's door I found my life again.] Vv. 61–66, 74–84; pp. 327–328 in *D'Aubigné: Oeuvres*, Pleiade edition

There is more precision of time and place in a similar account of spiritual rebirth given in *Les Fers* of *Les Tragiques*. The text is set in a cumbersome fiction, the poet narrating the battles and tribulations of his coreligionists as if he were prophesying them. To authenticate his visions he describes how he came to have them after he had been severely wounded at the time of the fourth war (i.e., in the campaigns that followed the Saint Bartholomew massacre):

Parmi ces aspres temps l'esprit, ayant laissé
Aux assassins mon corps en divers lieux percé,

> Par l'Ange consolant mes ameres blessures,
> Bien qu'impur, fut mené dans les regions pures.

[In those dreadful days my spirit, having abandoned to its killers my body pierced with blows, was taken, although unworthy, by an angel who, consoling my bitter wounds, led me to the heavens above.]

The poet then views a succession of celestial visions, after which the consoling angel turns to his spirit with these admonitions:

> "Retourne à ta moitié, n'attache plus ta veue
> Au loisir de l'Eglise, au repos de Capue.
> Il te faut retourner satisfaict en ton lieu,
> Employer ton bras droict aux vengeances de Dieu.
> Je t'ay guidé au cours du celeste voyage,
> Escrits fidellement: que jamais autre ouvrage,
> Bien que plus delicat, ne te semble plaisant
> Au prix des hauts secrets du firmament luisant.
> Ne chante que de Dieu, n'oubliant que lui mesme
> T'a retiré: voilà ton corps sanglant et blesme
> Recueilly à Thalcy, sur une table, seul,
> A qui on a donné pour suaire un linceul.
> Rapporte luy la vie en l'amour naturelle
> Que, son masle, tu dois porter à ta femelle."
>   Tu m'as monstré, ô Dieu, que celuy qui te sert
> Sauve sa vie alors que pour toy il la perd.
> Ta main m'a delivré, je te sacre la mienne,
> Je remets en ton sein cette ame qui est tienne.

["Now return to your other half, look no longer on the peace of the church, on the repose of Capua. Content, you must return to your place and wield your right arm for the wrath of God. I have guided you in this heavenly path, so write faithfully; may no other work, for all its charm, be pleasing to you when compared to the lofty secrets of the shining firmament. Sing only of God, forgetting not that He Himself brought you back: there is your body, bloody and pale, laid out in Talcy, on a table, alone, with a sheet for a shroud. Take back to it the life which, in natural love, you must, as the male, bear for your female."

Thou hast shown me, O God, that he who serves Thee saves his life when for Thee he loses it. Thy hand has delivered me, I consecrate mine to Thee, and lay on Thy breast this soul which is Thine.] Vv. 1195–1198; 1417–1434; p. 184, *D'Aubigné: Oeuvres*, Pléiade edition

The clear reference to Talcy, supported by the two-day period of unconsciousness noted in the *Elégie*, argues that the conversion followed the attack on d'Aubigné at the inn and his desperate ride back to the castle so that he might die in the arms of Diane Salviati. Through fear, dejection, estrangement, he was psychologically conditioned for a religious conversion. And it was soon after made firm by the undisturbed isolation in which he lived through the winter, spring, and early summer of 1572–1573 at his house in Les Landes, a retreat which he left only when he was summoned by Henry of Navarre to Paris, and to a life of devoted service.

Notes

1. These were the surviving children of d'Aubigné's marriage to Suzanne de Lezay. There were two other sons, Agrippa and Henri, who died in infancy, and an illegitimate son, Nathan, who was devoted to his father and followed him into exile in Geneva.
2. After his assassination in 1610, Henry IV was popularly honored with the title Henry the Great. François de Fayolles, lord of Neuvy, was one of Henry's lieutenants in the campaigns of the 1580s.

CHAPTER I

1. In fact 1552, since it was still customary to begin the year at Easter time. D'Aubigné's parents and genealogy are discussed at length in Armand Garnier's biography, *Agrippa d'Aubigné et le parti protestant*, 3 vols. (Paris, 1928), 1:3–31.
2. Jean d'Aubigné married Anne de Limur soon after the death of his first wife; they had three children. Agrippa in the meantime was taken first to Archiac, twelve miles southwest of Pons, to the home of Aubin d'Abeville, husband of Jean's niece, and later to the house of Antoinette d'Albret in Pons, where legend tells that he played on occasion with the young Henry of Navarre, one year his junior.

3. Cottin was an evangelical zealot; he died at the stake in Rouen in 1569.

4. These were the victims of the Tumult or Conspiracy of Amboise (March–April 1560), arising from a Huguenot plot to abduct the young king Francis II. Louis de Bourbon, the first prince of Condé, was behind it as a means of checking the ambitions of the Guise, who appeared to be in full control at court and who had staked a claim to the leadership of the Catholic cause in the face of growing Protestant strength. Condé, who had embraced the new religion, looked to the Huguenot gentry, to men like Jean d'Aubigné, for the means to counter them. The plot thus born was actually organized and led by Jean du Barry, sieur de La Renaudie, who did not keep its secrets well. The conspirators were arrested as they rode to Amboise, where the king was in protective residence, and the leaders were hanged or beheaded. The text indicates that their bodies were still on display several weeks afterward.

5. This was two years later, April 1562, and he stayed in Paris only two months. Mathieu Béroalde was a humanist, related to Vatable by marriage, and a convert to Protestantism. Since 1555 he had taken pupils into his house for instruction, among them Pierre de L'Estoile, future author of the *Mémoires-Journaux*.

6. Condé seized Orleans on April 2, 1562, an action that marked the beginning of the first war of religion and that led to the royal edicts of May 26 and 27, which ordered the expulsion of Protestants from Paris. The war resulted from a series of events going back to the death of Francis II in December 1560, and the accession to the throne of his eleven-year-old brother Charles IX. The queen mother, Catherine de Médicis, assumed the regency and with her chancellor, Michel de L'Hospital, adopted a policy of toleration to calm the religious conflicts among her subjects. To this end she sponsored the Colloquy of Poissy (August–October 1561), a debate between Catholic and Protestant theologians intended to resolve their

differences. It had the opposite effect. But Catherine was impressed by the Protestant presence and by the eloquence and charm of Théodore de Bèze, Calvin's heir-apparent in Geneva and leader of the Protestant delegation to Poissy. Persuaded of the near-equal strength of the two religions, she issued the Edict of January (1562), which granted generous conditions of religious freedom. But these concessions aroused the Catholics. They also spurred the duke of Guise, Montmorency, and Saint-André to settle their personal differences and to form an alliance, popularly called the triumvirate, to oppose what they perceived to be the weakness of the court. There followed soon after the massacre at Vassy, where Guise's soldiers fired on Protestants who had assembled in a barn for religious services, and the strong protests of this event by Condé and Bèze before the court at Fontainebleau. Catherine then appealed to Condé to protect her and her son from Guise. But the triumvirs acted quickly and forced the court to return to the Catholic security of Paris. Condé then took Orleans and proclaimed himself the protector of the king.

The war, which lasted until March 1563, was marked by innumerable atrocities committed by each side. German troops supported Condé's army in Orleans, and an English force occupied Le Havre according to the treaty of Hampton Court by which Queen Elizabeth agreed to support the Huguenots in exchange for Calais. The major battle was at Dreux (December 1562), a royal victory in which Saint-André was killed and the opposing commanders, Montmorency and Condé, were taken prisoner. Two months later at the siege of Orleans, Guise was shot and killed from ambush (February 17, 1563).

7. According to Béroalde's journal, quoted by Garnier (*Agrippa d'Aubigné*, 1:47), Achon was simply a brigand; Democarès, on the other hand, was Antoine de Mouchy, rector of the University of Paris.

8. Renée de France, daughter of Louis XII and wife of Ercole d'Este, duke of Ferrara. She had deep sympathies for the re-

form movement and had made of her Italian court a sanctuary for its refugees. Since 1559 she had resided in Montargis, where she continued to welcome the persecuted.

9. Symphorien de Durfort, sieur de Duras, was killed March 12, 1563, the day the peace agreement was signed.

10. Montmorency had been captured at Dreux.

11. With the leaders of the opposing factions killed or captured, Catherine de Médicis, queen mother and regent, had come herself to Orleans to negotiate the peace. It was followed by the Edict of Amboise, which restricted the liberties previously accorded to the Protestants by the Edict of January.

12. This was a councillor of the parlement who received petitions from private parties and relayed them directly to the royal chancellor.

13. The same who had cared for d'Aubigné when he was an infant; he was his uncle by marriage to Jean d'Aubigné's sister.

14. Theodore de Bèze (1519–1604), was one of the great Protestant leaders. Born in France, converted to the reform movement, he fled to Switzerland in 1548, where he taught in Lausanne and served on many diplomatic and religious missions like the Colloquy of Poissy. He succeeded Calvin at the latter's death (1564) as pastor in Geneva, rector of its college, and virtual leader of the Calvinist movement.

Orbilius was the stern schoolmaster described by Horace (*Epistles*, 2.1.70–71).

15. D'Aubigné, like an early Rousseau, seems to have left Geneva out of boredom. However, Eugénie Droz, in a note "Le Premier Séjour d'Agrippa d'Aubigné à Genève" (*Bibliothèque d'Humanisme et Renaissance*, 1947, pp. 169–173), reported from the archives of the city "une affaire autrement plus grave" which may account for his departure. He and another pupil at the college, also from Saintonge, were implicated in a charge of sodomy brought against a third boy, Bartholomé Tecia, fifteen, from Piedmont. The severity of the interrogations and the torture and condemnation to death by drowning of

the unfortunate Tecia give a direct cause for d'Aubigné's flight.

16. In a series of letters addressed to "M. de la Rivière, premier médecin du roi" (*Agrippa d'Aubigné: Oeuvres,* ed. Henri Weber, Bibliothèque de la Pléiade [Paris, Gallimard, 1969] pp. 835–851), d'Aubigné reviewed and commented upon the occult arts, magic, alchemy, witchcraft, etc. In the fifth letter (pp. 843–845) he described in detail his experiences in Lyons with a certain Louis d'Arza, who claimed to be a magician and from whom d'Aubigné learned a number of tricks with which he later baffled or mystified people.

17. The admiral (commander of the king's sea forces, at that time an honorary but still prestigious appointment) was Gaspard de Coligny, Montmorency's nephew and one of the great Huguenot captains. He had supported Condé in the first war and campaigned effectively in Normandy. At this time he was corresponding with John Casimir, son of King Frederick III of Bavaria, to secure German support for the next uprising. Duke Casimir, as d'Aubigné will call this zealous and rapacious Calvinist, was to lead many invasions into France.

18. The second war began in the autumn of 1566 and lasted until the Peace of Longjumeau of the following March. Its cause, against a background of unrelieved tensions between the religious groups, would seem to have been the uprising of the Low Countries against Spain that began in 1565. The early successes of the Dutch Calvinists ignited scattered outbursts of Huguenot bands in France. In these explosive conditions Condé and Coligny tried unsuccessfully to abduct the king at Meaux. Catherine had to face the collapse of her policy of moderation.

19. The third war, the bloodiest in terms of battle casualties and gratuitous atrocities, began in September 1568 and lasted until the Peace of Saint-Germain in August 1570. During the brief truce that followed the preceding war it became known that Condé and Coligny were negotiating with William of Orange, leader of the Dutch revolt, to combine their forces against

Spain. Fearing that this would involve France in a war against the redoubtable Philip II, Catherine tried to arrest the Huguenot leaders. They retreated to the southwest, the center of their strength, and issued their call to arms. D'Aubigné, now in Saintonge, was well placed to heed it.

20. D'Aubigné here would have been armed with a harquebus, a primitive firearm with a mechanism that held a slow-burning match to ignite the powder charge. Before battle a soldier designated for the task would light the matches for all the men thus armed.

21. Pons was taken in October 1568. In the *Histoire* (5.5.33–34) d'Aubigné tells that four hundred royalist soldiers were massacred after the capture of the city.

22. Jazeneuil, southwest of Poitiers, was the scene of bitter but indecisive fighting between the troops of Condé and the duke of Anjou, Charles IX's younger brother, whose courage and gallantry in this war gave false promise for his later reign as Henry III. La Rocheabeille (June 1569) was a victory for the Huguenots, which they followed up by taking Châtellerault and Lusignan and by laying siege to Poitiers. Many of the nobles took advantage of the siege to go home and look after their affairs; d'Aubigné took leave also, but to wage guerrilla warfare in the south.

   The Huguenots were beaten at Jarnac (March 1569), where Condé was murdered, and Moncontour (October 1569), where Anjou decisively beat Coligny. This victory gave Catherine the illusion that the rebellion had been crushed and she waited for a surrender. Instead, Coligny demonstrated his leadership by successfully retreating with his shattered forces into the south. With his army intact he was able to negotiate the next peace from a position of strength.

23. This is a faulty recollection of the tenth verse of Psalm 32 in Clément Marot's translation: "L'homme endurcy sera dompté de mesmes / Par maulx etc." *Oeuvres complètes*, ed. C. A. Mayer. (Geneva: Slatkine, 1980), 6:388. The Revised Standard Version

renders the verse: "Many are the pangs of the wicked. . . ."

24. Perhaps in sonnet 3 of *L'Hécatombe à Diane* in d'Aubigné's *Printemps*, where the conventional image of love as a storm at sea seems enhanced by the remembered pain of an exhausted swimmer.

25. *Bisogne*, a clown or scoundrel, was a name given to recruits. The prince of Condé here would be Henry I, no older than d'Aubigné.

26. These *enfants perdus* were assault troops. Philippe Aries cites the term as an example of the imprecision of the word *enfant* in the past (*Centuries of Childhood*, trans. Robert Baldick [New York: Knopf, 1962], p. 27).

27. Boisrond's horse cleared an earthen rampart with one bound and threw panic among the defenders (*Histoire*, 5.25.185).

28. Pons was d'Aubigné's home town. With only twenty-five men he crept up to the walls under cover of darkness, hailed a man in a window, and persuaded him to throw the keys to one of the gates down to him (*Histoire*, 5.28.204–205).

29. For d'Aubigné's spiritual change see Appendix B.

CHAPTER 2

1. The Peace of Saint-Germain was signed August 8, 1570. D'Aubigné's property, inherited from his mother, was at Les Landes near Mer, equidistant from Blois and Beaugency on the right bank of the Loire.

2. Diane was the daughter of Jean and the granddaughter of Bernard Salviati. The latter had come to France with Catherine de Médicis at the time of her marriage. He bought the castle of Talcy, and Jean later embellished it with Italianate refinements. It is located approximately twelve kilometers north-northwest of Les Landes. D'Aubigné here passes quickly over the love affair, but the poetry in *Le Printemps* that it inspired, *L'Hécatombe à Diane* and most of *Les Stances*, shows it to have been an authentic, and devastating, emotional experience.

3. This was the extent of d'Aubigné's personal involvement in the Flemish project, a Huguenot scheme to support the rebellion of the Netherlands against Spain. The rebellion, begun in 1565, was a complex affair, nationalistic in origin, but with enough economic and religious implications to invite international interest. By 1572 England, German Protestant states, and the French Huguenots had formed a loose league to support the Dutch and the Flemings in the happy prospect of injuring Spain to their own political or economic advantage. To advance the Huguenot contribution to the plan, Coligny, now the effective leader of the Protestant party in France, let himself be persuaded to rejoin the royal court in September 1571. There his intelligence and moral probity soon won the mind and heart of the young Charles IX. But the king's sudden devotion to Coligny and the rash commitments he was prepared to make to support the Dutch rebellion and thus antagonize Spain aroused Catherine's deepest concern and may well have convinced her to get rid of the admiral.

In May 1572 Louis of Nassau, who had been in France to deal with Huguenot leaders, marched with fifteen hundred men into Flanders and occupied Mons and Valenciennes. They were soon besieged by Spanish troops under the relentless Duke of Alba. By the end of June, Valenciennes had been retaken by him and the situation at Mons was becoming desperate. Coligny persuaded Charles to send a relief expedition, which on July 17 was virtually annihilated by the Spanish. D'Aubigné was evidently involved in plans to raise another relief column.

4. One of Catherine's schemes to keep the peace was to marry her daughter Marguerite to Henry of Navarre, prince of the blood and titular leader of the Huguenot party. The marriage took place August 18. It and the military preparations for Flanders account for the large number of Huguenots in Paris at that time.

5. The massacre of Saint Bartholomew's Day, the most famous,

or infamous, of the atrocities that scar that troubled time, began with the wounding of Coligny on the afternoon of Friday, August 22, as he was walking to his house for dinner. The next day, to the ringing of the bells of Saint-Germain-L'Auxerrois, a mob invaded his house, killed him, and threw his body down into the street. Then the general slaughter began. The concerted nature of the massacre, the number of its victims, its rapid spread to other cities, all argue for a well-planned plot, responsibility for which is generally laid on Catherine and the Guise, with only the nature and extent of their complicity left for debate. D'Aubigné painted a vivid tableau of the massacre in *Les Tragiques: Fers* (vv. 765–1190), but on the testimony of others, for he escaped the massacre by his fortuitous flight to avoid arrest. Henry of Navarre was safe in the Louvre, where he would remain a prisoner until his escape in 1576; under the circumstances he prudently abjured his Protestantism.

6. Sancerre and La Rochelle were the principal cities in which the leaderless Huguenots sought refuge and made their resistance.

7. Michel de L'Hospital (1505–1573), lawyer and statesman, had served as chancellor of France from 1560 to 1568, when he tried to implement Catherine's original policy of reconciliation of the religious factions, which of course earned for him the hostility of each. This policy collapsed with the second war, and at the outbreak of the third war he was dismissed. D'Aubigné in his *Histoire* (2.18.272–273) asserted that he was involved in the Conspiracy of Amboise.

8. Despite the cavalier tone in which d'Aubigné describes it, this incident probably induced his conversion. See appendix B.

9. The chevalier de Salviati, grand master of the Knights Hospitaler of Saint Lazarus, was Diane's uncle. His intolerance alone could explain the rupture of the marriage plans, but the love poetry indicates that it was Diane herself who rejected her lover. It is also plausible that the Salviati family had simply

used her to extract as much information as could be had from d'Aubigné, and that by this time they had no further need of him.

10. Guillaume Postel (1510–1581) was a famous physician as well as a devotee of arcane mystical speculation. It was at this time of isolation and depression that d'Aubigné composed the grim poems of despair in *Les Stances*.

11. The Peace of La Rochelle, followed by the Edict of Boulogne, ended the fourth war, which had begun with the fighting incited by the Saint Bartholomew massacre. The principal actions were fought in the royal sieges of Sancerre and La Rochelle. Mutual exhaustion at the latter city led to the truce signed in July 1573.

Just before that time the duke of Anjou learned of the success of his candidacy for the throne of Poland, and he went there to reign until the death of Charles IX the following year. His departure raised the status of the youngest brother, Francis, duke of Alençon, a restless youth of sixteen who aspired to supplant the dashing Henry and to rival the sickening Charles. It is significant that d'Aubigné here already refers to him as "Monsieur," the title reserved to the heir to the throne.

The intrigues of Alençon and of Henry of Navarre, still under house arrest, were stimulated by the knowledge that the Huguenot party had recovered rapidly from the loss of its leaders in the massacre. The inherently democratic tendencies of the original religious movement, lost when a discontented nobility assumed leadership, now reasserted themselves, and took a political form with the establishment of bodies to provide civil administration, collect taxes, wage war, and assure security. This political development was accompanied by an ideological one, the formulation of ideas that questioned the claims of monarchy, denounced tyranny, and advocated constitutional procedures to assure liberty and judicial reponsibility. Such ideas found fertile ground among the oppressed Protestants, and they appealed to moderate and disaffected

Catholics as well. The latter came to be called *politiques* because they seemed to be prepared to separate political from religious ends. The sons of Montmorency (Damville, Thoré, and Méru), jealous of the return to favor of the Guise since the fall of L'Hospital, sensed the power of the new movement, captured its leadership, and had the brilliant idea of giving it a cover of legitimacy by calling upon Alençon to be its chief.

The first project of the new coalition was the plot to free Alençon and Navarre from the court and, under the threat of a renewal of civil war, to dictate terms to the government. An attack on the court at Saint-Germain was planned for March 1574. It miscarried, and Alençon was arrested and revealed the names of the conspirators. Most of them escaped, but his friends Coconas and Boniface de La Mole (whose memory was revered by Mathilde de La Mole in Stendhal's *The Red and the Black*) were caught and executed.

12. D'Aubigné went to court in the late summer of 1573, where he observed the festivities to honor the Polish ambassadors who had come to escort their new king back to Poland. His nomination as squire to Henry of Navarre may have been made then but kept secret until the following spring, when Montgomery, the luckless count who had accidentally killed Henry II in a joust and fled to England, where he converted to Protestantism, landed in Normandy with English troops to provoke a new war. This may have been part of the broad uprising planned in the conspiracy of the *politiques* to intimidate the government.

13. Navarre was more closely guarded than ever because of his suspected involvement in the plot to free him. Sending d'Aubigné off to the war in Normandy would appear to be a gesture of loyalty.

Guillaume de Hautemer, lord of Fervacques, served under Matignon, who had been sent to Normandy to suppress Montgomery's invasion. As a favorite of Alençon, Fervacques found it easy to rally later to Navarre.

14. In the *Histoire* (7.7.244) d'Aubigné asserted, as if to justify his service in the Catholic army, that he tried to save Montgomery under Navarre's orders and with the cooperation of Fervacques.

15. Charles IX died May 30, 1574. On learning the news, his brother left Poland to claim the throne of France. He was crowned Henry III in February 1575.

16. Perhaps to minimize his service in the royal, i.e., Catholic, armies, d'Aubigné has telescoped the period between the Normandy campaign, which ended with the capture of Montgomery on May 26, 1574, and the battles of Archecourt and Dormans in the fall of 1575. The latter followed a series of events that began with the flight of Alençon from the court in September 1574 and his issuance of a manifesto in which he proclaimed himself defender of the public good and appealed for the support of the disaffected elements of all the parties. This launched the fifth war and brought forth a new generation of faction leaders. In response to Alençon's call Montmorency-Thoré, a refugee in Germany since the collapse of the conspiracy of the *politiques* in March 1574, joined the new prince of Condé, also in Germany where he was enlisting an army, and led an advance force into France. To counter them, the new duke of Guise marched eastward with a royal army to which d'Aubigné was attached. The battles that d'Aubigné cites were fought in eastern France in October and November 1575. It was at Dormans that Guise received the wound that won him the nickname *le balafré* and made of him a national hero.

17. *Circe* was written for the festivities to honor the Polish ambassadors in 1573. In the *Histoire* (11.14.118) d'Aubigné said that the cost of its production was estimated at 300,000 crowns.

18. The Chapeau Rouge was a tavern on the rue du Comte d'Artois near the church of Saint-Eustache.

19. Louis de Clermont, Lord of Bussy, was one of the bright young men whom Henry III favored for his inner circle. The duel with Fervacques was apparently fought for the honor of

Queen Marguerite, of whom Bussy at that time was a lover. But the story is more complex: when Marguerite seduced Bussy she drew him away from Henry III, with whom she had quarreled, and into the entourage of Alençon. The king, annoyed, reported the affair to her husband, Navarre, who laughed it off. Fervacques then assumed the duty of defending his master's honor. The duel was a draw, so a night attack was made on Bussy, who escaped with a slight wound. This last incident seems to have convinced Alençon to leave the court and launch his movement.

20. Françoise de Beaune de Montreval, widow of Carnavalet, was Fervacques's cousin. She bought the house which is now the Musée Carnavalet in Paris.

21. These anecdotes reflect the enmities that characterized the court of Henry III. Guise, as the strong man of the court, was a principal target of intrigue.

22. These are the arrangements with Fervacques, Laverdin, and a few others that led to Navarre's escape from his princely captivity February 4, 1576. D'Aubigné's narrative skips the escape itself and resumes with the king and his companions in flight to their first refuge, the city of Alençon, where they were joined by 250 gentlemen.

23. Professional scribes set up shop near the cemetery and charnel house of Saints-Innocents in Paris to dash off epitaphs, some evidently like this one.

24. Navarre did not make a formal abjuration until June 1576. Uncertain of his place among Henry, who was proving to be a weak and unpopular king, Alençon, who claimed leadership of the malcontents, and Condé, official leader of the Huguenots, he probably wanted to keep his options open.

25. D'Aubigné had to content himself with this kind of guerrilla fighting because Navarre did not initiate any military action, nor did he join his fellow rebels Alençon, who led an army of Huguenots and Catholic malcontents, or Condé, who had brought in 20,000 *reîtres* under Duke Casimir. As a result he

was not associated with the atrocities committed by those armies.

The king of Navarre may also have known that Alençon was already involved in secret negotiations with the court that culminated in the Peace of Beaulieu (or *Paix de Monsieur*) of May 6, 1576. This put an end to the fifth war, but on terms so generous to the Huguenots and their leaders that there was widespread Catholic reaction, like the stubborn refusal of Picardy to accept Condé as governor as the treaty provided. And there a group of townsmen and clergy formed the Holy League to oppose not only Protestantism but also a king who could make what they considered to be outrageous concessions. The new movement soon covered much of France. Henry III, himself resentful of the treaty forced upon him, did not resist the League but tried to harness its volatile energies for his own ends.

26. Indeed, Jeanne de Tignonville resisted Navarre's attentions until after her marriage in 1581.

27. The companions who planned Navarre's escape from the court had sworn an oath of hatred against any of their number who reneged; the oath had been sealed with a kiss.

28. Charles Eschallart de La Boulaye and Louis de Saint-Gelais, lord of Lusignan, were close friends of d'Aubigné and will return in his story.

29. Catherine de Bourbon, sister of Henry of Navarre.

CHAPTER 3

1. This was an important mission. Because of the Catholic reaction to the Peace of Beaulieu and the incitements of the League, the coalition of Huguenots and Catholic malcontents began to crack. Alençon was enticed back to court and many of the Catholic gentry who had rallied to Henry of Navarre began to slip away. The Huguenots themselves were split by the leadership offered by Condé, who claimed the allegiance

of the radicals, and of Navarre, who was trying to maintain his coalition. D'Aubigné's mission was to ascertain the latter's scattered support.

2. As a result of the manipulations of the League the delegates to this assembly of the States General were almost all Catholics. Mirambeau was one of the few Protestants in attendance, and evidently the only one to speak. The speech d'Aubigné claims to have prepared for him pleaded for peace and for conformity to the current treaty, but the States voted for religious unity, and this launched the sixth war.

3. This passage is confusing because there are three Saint-Gelais's involved: the castle of Saint-Gelais, northeast of Niort and the stronghold of d'Aubigné's friend, Louis de Saint-Gelais, and the Saint-Gelais gate in the city of Niort, where the attack was made.

   Damville, eldest of Montmorency's sons, was governor of Languedoc. He was a Catholic but followed a policy of toleration with his substantial Protestant population, and this cast him in the role of an independent. In 1575 he had rallied to Alençon and thus appeared to be part of the coalition that Navarre was trying to preserve. At this time he was zealously courted by the two Henrys.

4. François de La Noue, Bras-de-Fer (1531–1591), was one of the leading Huguenot captains.

5. The "affairs in Languedoc" centered on the uncertain allegiance of Damville, whose independent policies were described briefly in note 3 above. Navarre sent d'Aubigné to see Damville to keep him from reaching an agreement with Henry III. When d'Aubigné arrived the agreement had already been made, but he was still able to learn the names of the Catholic gentlemen at the court of Navarre who were conspiring with the court of France. These are the *infidèles* whose names d'Aubigné divulged on his return, to the jeopardy of Navarre's wish to maintain his coalition. This would have angered the king, but d'Aubigné probably exaggerates when he says that it led to the decision to have him killed.

6. His adversary was Laverdin, a Catholic gentleman who assisted in Navarre's escape from Paris and who had remained in his service. But d'Aubigné was suspicious of him and had identified him as one of the *infidèles*, and this led to their quarrel. The duel was really an ambush, and d'Aubigné's friends stopped it.

7. This was as lieutenant to the governor of Castel-Jaloux, Vachonière.

8. François de La Magdaleine was another Catholic gentleman in Navarre's service. He was a redoubtable swordsman who would have assisted Laverdin in the thwarted duel with d'Aubigné.

9. "Young Bacoue" was a younger brother of the man who was killed in the fight recounted in the passage from the *Histoire* quoted above.

10. Even though he had refused the governorship of Castel-Jaloux, d'Aubigné assumed effective command and, rapidly recovered from his wounds, resumed his guerrilla activity, of which the taking of Castelnau provides an example. Such independence of action was, however, an embarrassment to Navarre, whose forces were being beaten back in the north and who was trying to negotiate a peace with the government. In these circumstances, it is plausible that he would offer Villars a free hand to retake Castelnau.

11. The Peace of Bergerac, signed in September 1577 and confirmed by the Edict of Poitiers, ended the sixth war. It restricted the rights and privileges accorded to the Protestants by the Peace of Beaulieu, but was still an effective compromise that anticipated the provisions of the Edict of Nantes. D'Aubigné, however, was bitterly disappointed with it, and spent the next two years away from the court in a sulk.

12. In fact, only Saint-Gelais lived near Bougouin, Suzanne's residence east of Niort, and d'Aubigné did not court her seriously for the next two years. Until September 1579 he remained for the most part at his house at Les Landes, where he wrote the first books of *Les Tragiques*.

13. D'Aubigné broke the quiet of his retreat at Les Landes with this and other adventures in anticipation of the next campaigns.

CHAPTER 4

1. Demogorgon was an earth spirit whom alchemists identified with life or growth.

2. This was the seventh war: its popular name, *la guerre des amoureux*, is apparently due to d'Aubigné, who in the *Histoire* (9.5.382–386) ascribed its cause to the amorous intrigues of Henry, Marguerite, Turenne, and others. In fact, it was caused by the refusal of the Huguenots to surrender certain cities as stipulated in the conference of Nerac, where Henry and Catherine had met early in 1579 to settle the problems that troubled the peace. It was there that Marguerite rejoined her husband. The war was of little consequence and ended six months later with the Peace of Fleix (November 1580), which reaffirmed the Peace of Bergerac.

3. D'Aubigné introduced and concluded his account of the adventure at Limoges as a lesson in the need for careful planning and sound intelligence in a military operation.

4. Montaigu was a stategically important city south of Nantes; d'Aubigné and La Boulaye captured it in April 1580 and held it against repeated attacks.

5. Blaye, on the Gironde, was to be taken with the collusion of certain of its defenders. But the plan fell through, unknown to d'Aubigné, who arrived when his own men were about to withdraw and the defenders were on full alert. He attacked anyway and had to retreat in disorder.

6. Armand de Gontaut, baron of Biron, commanded the royal army in Guyenne. Navarre made a brave show to oppose him at the outbreak of the war, but his people did not rise up to support him and he had to retreat into his southern strongholds. In the summer of 1580 Biron was methodically picking these off. In September he marched on Nerac, evidently not

145

to attack the city but to humiliate the king of Navarre. This situation explains the background of fear and gloom for d'Aubigné's quixotic show of resistance.

7. Albanian cavalry served as mercenary troops in the royal armies; they were renowned for their horsemanship.

8. Guy de Daillon, count of Lude, commanded the royal troops besieging Montaigu. When the peace was signed he summoned d'Aubigné to discuss which side should proclaim it.

9. The king and queen of Navarre, the prince of Condé, and Alençon were together at Libourne and the castle of Cadillac in January and February 1581 to decide the implementation of the Peace of Fleix. At issue was the exchange of strongholds held by each side to restore the *status quo ante*. However, the situation was complicated by affairs in the Iberian Peninsula and the Spanish Netherlands. Two years before, the king of Portugal had been killed, leaving no direct heir to his throne. Philip II seized the opportunity and claimed it for himself. A Portuguese pretender, Dom Antonio, then came to France to seek support for himself against Philip. At first he pursued his interests with Alençon, who at this time had become involved in the Netherlands rebellion by joining forces with William of Orange. Against this background the queen of Navarre proposed to d'Aubigné that he cultivate Antonio's constable, Francisco, count of Vimioso, who happened to be at Cadillac at the time, and persuade him that Portuguese interests would be better served with the king of Navarre. D'Aubigné, whose relations with Marguerite had always been strained, and who at this very time had made known her liaison with Jacques de Harlay, had serious reason to question her motives.

10. Loro was a Spanish officer who sought a meeting with Navarre to discuss a plan to turn over to him the fort of Fontarabia. D'Aubigné suspected an assassination attempt and kept him at a distance until he was arrested, tortured into a confession, and executed (*Histoire*, 10.5.182–187).

11. Lansac and Aubeterre were both royalist officers attached to the court of Navarre.

12. This incident would have occurred early in 1581 when the princes were gathered in Cadillac. François de Candalle (1502–1594), a member of the family that owned the castle, was the bishop of Aire and a noted mathematician and scholar.

13. Marguerite had been invited back to Paris in the hope that her husband would follow as a sign of national reconciliation. The queen mother came as far as Saint-Maixent to meet her daughter.

14. The *sfrisata*, or affront, was an attack on Madame de Duras, one of Marguerite's attendants, who was slapped and hit with a bottle of ink when she left the queen's room one evening. This Clermont d'Amboise was probably Bussy's younger brother, Georges, Bussy having been killed in 1579.

15. Claude-Catherine de Clermont-Dampierre (1545–1603), maréchale de Retz, wife of Albert de Gondi, and related to d'Aubigné's future wife, was a learned lady celebrated by the poets for her "salon de Dictynne," which flourished about 1570 in her house in the Faubourg Saint-Honore in Paris. She also played the sexual games of the type alleged here, which inspired the *Divorce satyrique* ascribed to d'Aubigné and published in volume 2 of the *Oeuvres complètes*. Entragues, François de Balzac, was the husband of Marie Touchet, mistress of Charles IX, and father of Henriette de Balzac d'Entragues, marquise de Verneuil, who would be the last of the recognized mistresses of Henry IV.

16. This was a popular belief adopted as a poetic conceit to deal with the hardness of a lady's heart.

17. The king slept in Saint-Maixent and commuted to La Mothe-Sainte-Heraye, where discussions with Catherine took place. But for the gossips, d'Aubigné would appear to have left as the queen wished.

18. Suzanne de Lezay, the wealthy and well-born young lady whom d'Aubigné first met in 1577. See above, chapter 3.

19. No trace remains of these documents.

20. The marriage took place June 6, 1583. Suzanne's dowry included the domain of Surimeau and the castle of Mursay, where they would live. Both properties are close to Niort. The castle today is in an advanced state of decay.

CHAPTER 5

1. Marguerite had been ill-used in Paris, for when Navarre failed to follow her she lost her value as a lure. Henry III banished her unceremoniously in August 1583 when he learned that she was dealing with Alençon. On her way out of Paris her carriage was stopped by an officer of the guard who tore the masks off the faces of two of her ladies.

2. D'Aubigné was sent to Paris to make a formal protest of the treatment of the queen of Navarre. In his account in the *Histoire* (10.3.171–172) he quotes himself as speaking bluntly to the king, who replied in kind and made a threatening move with his dagger.

3. This was in August 1584. Alençon had died two months before, and Henry of Navarre thus became the heir presumptive to the throne of France. In recognition of this development, Henry III dispatched the duke of Epernon to his cousin to urge a reconciliation and to persuade him to convert to Catholicism and come to the royal court.

   Garnier (*Agrippa d'Aubigné*, 1:301–303) found confusion in d'Aubigné's recollections here, since at the time of Epernon's visit to Nerac, Ségur was on an extended diplomatic mission among the Protestant princes. Garnier was inclined, therefore, to place the incident two years earlier, when Navarre was being pressed by the king and by Marguerite to return to the royal court.

4. Diane d'Andouins, widow of the count of Guiche and known as "la belle Corisande," had been Navarre's mistress since 1581.

5. Nicolas Dortoman, vice-chancellor of the University of Montpellier and physician to Henry of Navarre, was highly re-

garded by d'Aubigné, who did indeed consult him about love potions (*Lettres sur diverses sciences*, pp. 845–848 of *D'Aubigné: Oeuvres*, Pléiade edition).

6. After her expulsion from Paris, Marguerite had become a pawn in a diplomatic game played by the two kings; she was allowed to return to Nerac on April 13, 1584.

7. These marriages involved strategically important land holdings. D'Aubigné bought Le Chaillou, near Melle, shortly before his marriage to match the substantial dowry of his bride. Condé acquired Taillebourg on the Charente by his marriage to Charlotte de La Trémoille in 1586.

8. The new war was provoked by the belligerence of the League. The force of the movement had waned after the Peace of Bergerac, but with the death of Alençon and the promotion of Henry of Navarre to the role of heir presumptive, the League revived with greater energy and purpose than before. Guise assumed leadership and allied the party to Spain by the Treaty of Joinville (December 1584). Among the agreements were the extirpation of heresy in France and the Low Countries, the exclusion of Navarre from the royal succession, and the recognition of Charles Cardinal de Bourbon as heir to the throne of France. With generous Spanish subsidies Guise proceeded to create a virtual state within the state, not unlike the Huguenot model. Henry III recognized the danger to the kingdom and tried to enlist Navarre's support for the legitimate monarchy. But the latter would not, or could not, yet pay the price of conversion.

   On March 21, 1585, Guise seized Châlons-sur-Marne, made of it his headquarters, and issued his *Manifeste de Peronne*, an open challenge to Henry III. The latter squirmed, but lacking popular support and almost bankrupt, he was obliged to capitulate in July with the Treaty of Nemours, implemented by the Edict of July. The effect of the edict was to revoke all existing edicts of religious toleration and to proscribe Protestantism in France. The eighth war began.

The revival of the League made legitimists of the Huguenots but raised the question of whether they should support the monarchy by joining the royal armies against the League or by maintaining their independence as a separate party. The latter course was adopted at the conference of Guîtres at the end of May.

The war began with unusual caution on all sides. Henry III's financial distress prevented him from taking the field. Henry of Navarre was willing to play a waiting game for the crown that would be his. And Guise, despite his aggressive words, seemed reluctant to challenge his king directly. Moreover, Philip II restrained him because it was in his interest to keep the crisis in France unresolved while he pursued Spanish objectives in the Netherlands and against England.

9. Mercoeur, one of the leaders of the League, led an army of Bretons into the southwest in the first major campaign of the war (July 1585). It was characterized by atrocities committed against civilians and prisoners.

10. The reformationists claimed that an article of the council dispensed Catholics from keeping promises made to heretics.

11. Condé, supported by a fleet, had settled down to the siege of Brouage, where Saint-Luc was in command. The defenders were so bottled up that he felt he could detach a portion of his army to go to the relief of the Huguenot force that had captured the castle of Angers even though the city remained in Catholic hands. In October 1585 his troops, imprudently transported to the north bank of the Loire, found themselves facing superior forces. His army had to scatter to avoid encirclement; he fled to England, and d'Aubigné, who remained to the last to direct the evacuation of his men, escaped by going upriver to Mer. In the meantime, the siege of Brouage was broken.

12. These operations took place in January and February 1586. Neither king wanted to pursue the war, but they could not control their zealots who undertook their own operations. To

the Huguenot radicals Navarre seemed to be temporizing, which explains the pressure on d'Aubigné to take the offensive that winter.

13. Condé, back from England in early 1586, had put Laval, a nephew of Coligny, in charge of the western armies. The latter wanted to take the island of Oleron to draw the royal fleet down from Normandy and destroy it.

14. In April 1586 Saint-Luc with a fleet of 50 ships arrived to challenge d'Aubigné's garrison.

15. Garnier (*Agrippa d'Aubigné*, 1:355) ascribed Navarre's petulance to his comparative poverty. One might also suspect that at that critical moment for the French monarchy, when the heir-presumptive was playing for higher stakes than control of the Atlantic ports and their trade, his patience for such adventures had worn thin.

16. D'Aubigné's success in beating off attacks may have left him overconfident and he often spared men from his garrison to take part in operations on the mainland. On the last such occasion Saint-Luc landed a sizable force, which the islanders hid in their houses. A feint was then staged to draw out what remained of the garrison. D'Aubigné went out with a few men to observe this action and was easily captured and taken as a prisoner to Brouage (*Histoire*, 11.6.57–58).

17. "These shrouded [sorrows] are not hidden from thee." A version in French, entitled "Prière de l'autheur, prisonnier de guerre et condanné à mort," is found on pp. 377–378 of *D'Aubigné: Oeuvres*, Pleiade edition.

18. Biron had been sent with a royal army to establish control over Poitou.

19. The island could not have been sold when it had been taken by force; d'Aubigné probably interpreted in a venal sense Navarre's acceptance of the fait accompli.

20. Panigarola, a Franciscan from Milan, had defended the Saint Bartholomew massacre. Edmund Campion was an English Jesuit trained at the college in Douai; in 1580 he returned to

England, exhorted Catholics to resist Elizabeth, and wrote the book, *Decem rationes*, against Protestantism; he was arrested and beheaded in 1581. Robert Bellarmine, an Italian Jesuit, was one of the major polemicists of the Counter-Reformation.

21. William Whitaker, a professor at Cambridge, wrote to refute Bellarmine; Sidbrand Lubert was a German theologian who wrote against Baronius.

22. During d'Aubigné's absence Navarre had been treating with Catherine. She was convinced that a period of peace would mollify the Protestants, so she proposed a truce on condition that Henry accept the Edict of July (which proscribed Protestantism) or, barring that, a truce of one year with the religious question left for a future meeting of the States General to resolve. Navarre could accept neither condition. They then agreed to meet again in early 1587, but Henry sent Turenne in his place. The latter urged on Catherine an alliance of the two kings against the League, but this Catherine had to refuse. The fanatics on both sides naturally viewed these conferences with suspicion and fear, which explains d'Aubigné's comment on the affairs of his party. Failure to reach an agreement at this time led to a resumption of fighting and the capture of Talmont on the Atlantic coast. This and other victories in Saintonge and Poitou encouraged the Huguenots and caused Henry III to send the duke of Joyeuse to the southwest to reestablish order.

23. The Scotsmen had come to France and joined the Huguenots in quest of adventure. D'Aubigné was put in command of them and led them into some spectacular minor actions (*Histoire*, II.14.124–126). Their exploits evidently pricked the vanity of the Albanians in Joyeuse's army, and they issued the challenge mentioned here. Nothing came of it.

24. To make arrangements for the private fight with the Albanians, d'Aubigné visited Joyeuse's headquarters and noted the deterioration of his army. His report of this encouraged Navarre to attack Joyeuse and to pursue him north to the Loire.

25. This was the battle of Coutras, October 20, 1587. During d'Aubigné's illness in the summer and fall an army of Germans, enlisted for Navarre's support, had entered France and was slowly marching toward the upper Loire. Navarre broke contact with Joyeuse, whom he had been harrassing and marched southward, as if to meet his allies. Joyeuse in turn broke camp and followed Navarre. It was at Coutras that Navarre turned and disposed his army for battle.
26. D'Aubigné advised reinforcement of the left flank with infantry. This was where Joyeuse's cavalry attacked, but it was exhausted from having ridden too far and was shattered by the Huguenot ranks.
27. Coutras was a great Huguenot victory, but it changed little in the scheme of things. Navarre made no effort to exploit his triumph militarily; indeed, he outraged his followers when he went off to visit his mistress shortly after the battle. But the king of Navarre was never a fool, and he must have known that the advantage he had won was illusory. Royal troops under Matignon were moving up from the south while the main strength of Henry III's army stood intact along the Loire. Navarre was in no way prepared to face such strength. Moreover, as Garrett Mattingly argued in *The Armada* (Boston: Houghton, Mifflin 1959), he may not have wanted to. In his study of the battle of Coutras (pp. 158–171), Mattingly saw it as part of a master plan designed by Henry III to fend off both the League and Spain in the summer of 1587: he would send the League forth to do battle with the heretics while he held the center with the royal army. Thus, the League captains, Joyeuse and Guise, went respectively to meet the Huguenots in the southwest and the *reîtres* in the east. If these captains were defeated, and humiliated, the king's objectives would be better served than by victories, for the League and its master, Spain posed a greater threat to the state than the Huguenots. If this was indeed the plan, it almost succeeded. The king stood with his army on the Loire and turned back

the Germans with bribes and diplomacy. Joyeuse pursued Navarre and was killed at Coutras. But in the east the plan miscarried. Guise was a mediocre general and did not dare face the Germans in open battle, so he contented himself with nipping at their right flank in a series of surprise attacks. These facile but inconsequential victories enhanced his popularity in Paris and made him appear to be a hero, even as Joyeuse had become a martyr. Henry III, who seemed to be resting on the Loire and treating with the enemy, would pay dearly for this loss of face to his rivals.

An intriguing footnote to Coutras is provided by the record of Navarre's visit shortly after the battle to the castle of Montaigne, where he dined and spent the night. There is regrettably no record of what transpired between him and his host, but that Montaigne left his cherished retirement to go to Paris the following spring (where he was briefly detained by the League) to follow Henry III in his flight to Chartres after the Day of the Barricades, and that he attended the meeting of the States General in Blois in the fall, suggest that the dinner was more than a casual courtesy.

28. This was the project to occupy the mouth of the Loire and the Breton land approaches. D'Aubigné is probably in error dating the plan from fifteen years earlier, but he did scout the area ten years before. See above, chap. 3, n. 13.

29. Philippe de Mornay, known as Du Plessis-Mornay (1549–1623), scholar, theologian, and statesman, served Navarre effectively as a diplomat in England and the Low Countries and in the reconciliation with Henry III.

30. The siege took place October 4–21, 1588. The city, situated along the Atlantic coast south of the Loire, would seem to fit into the Breton plan, but the time and effort to take it support d'Aubigné's strategy of giving priority to naval forces.

He has omitted here the two most dramatic events of that year, the Day of the Barricades (May 12–13) and the defeat of the Spanish Armada in August. They were related. The Day of the Barricades resulted from a carefully coordinated plan of Philip II, working through his ambassador in Paris, Mendoza, to use the League to assure French neutrality or cooperation for the benefit of the naval expedition to be thrown against England. League garrisons were to occupy Channel ports and the northern provinces, and Guise himself was to enter Paris and hold the king. The latter project looked easy, since the League dominated the municipal administration and was prepared to unleash a population resentful of the king and ripe for revolt. Thus, when Guise entered Paris on May 9, it was to a tumultuous hero's welcome. Henry III, aware of the developing plot, summoned troops loyal to him. Their arrival the night of May 11 ignited an uprising. Crowds flowed into the streets, threw up barricades, effectively immobilized the soldiers, and trapped the king in the Louvre. He managed to escape, but the city belonged to the triumphant League. Guise's satisfaction, however, was evidently tempered by the power of the forces that he had unleashed, for a popular commune sprang up. This had the effect of softening his demands on the king, even as the latter, in refuge in Chartres and appalled at the prospect of a triumphant Spain, was also willing to negotiate. But Guise had the upper hand, and it was the king who made the concessions in the Pact of Union they signed in July. Among other things he agreed to exclude Henry of Navarre from the succession and to call the States General into session in the fall in Blois. But as news of the defeat of the Armada came in, the king's spirits revived and he prepared to challenge Guise for the support of the states. All this time the state of civil war continued.

31. D'Aubigné discussed the same four roles for Navarre in the preface to the *Histoire*, 1:13.

32. "Monsieur" was the duke of Alençon. See note 3 above.

33. The attack on Niort began December 27; Guise had been killed in Blois on the king's orders on December 23. The murder precipitated the most serious constitutional crisis for the

French monarchy before the revolution. The king and Guise had both erred as they competed for support among the delegates of the States General in the fall of 1588. But the states had not met to be courted. The religious fanaticism of the League did not prevent it from nurturing ideas of limited monarchy and representative institutions. Many of the delegates saw themselves as legitimate spokesmen of the nation. Thus when Guise, to further his own ambitions, pressed them to continue the war against the Huguenots, the delegates agreed but demanded limitations of royal power as a condition of approving the necessary taxes. The king balked at this because it not only reduced his powers but also enhanced the prestige of his rival. The mistake of the two Henrys was to relegate the states to the role of spectator or instrument of their personal contest of will and pride. The mistake would cost Guise his life and the king his throne. Paris reacted violently to the news of Guise's death. The king was formally deposed and a near-revolution followed. Guise's brother Mayenne assumed leadership of the League and tried to maintain some order.

34. Arambure led the first attack, which breached the walls of Niort; d'Aubigné then launched the main attack. In the confusion of darkness his men and Arambure's mistook each other for the enemy (*Histoire*, 12.15.1–8).

35. D'Aubigné captured Maillezais on December 31, 1588. This turned out to be his long-coveted seigneury and he would keep it as a principal residence until he was forced to sell it in 1619.

36. The Huguenot garrison at La Garnache was holding firm against a royal army under the duke of Nevers. On January 4 Nevers opened negotiations with the besieged, arguing that the Huguenots and the royalists should join forces against the League. A capitulation was signed January 6 with a delay of eight days, either to execute it or to allow for the reinforcement of the garrison. Navarre wanted to exploit the latter pro-

vision and brought up a relief force. But he fell ill and entrusted the mission to Chastillon, who arrived too late to stay the surrender. He had to beat a retreat in the darkness.

37. While d'Aubigné rested at Maillezais in early 1589, Navarre advanced to the Loire and met Henry III at Plessis-les-Tours for a formal reconciliation and union of forces. The siege of Jargeau, east of Orleans, was their first joint operation. D'Aubigné had rejoined Navarre by this time and was present for the incident alluded to here (*Histoire*, 12.21.62–63). The combined armies next moved north to encircle Paris.

38. Henry III was stabbed by Jacques Clément at Saint-Cloud on August 1. The wound at first did not seem serious, but the king died that night, leaving Henry of Navarre king of France. However, on August 7 the League, in control of Paris and its *parlement*, proclaimed the cardinal de Bourbon the new king as Charles X. It was a foolish gesture because the cardinal, who had been Henry III's prisoner since the murder of Guise, now fell into Navarre's hands.

39. D'Aubigné's advice, for which he is the only witness, is quoted in the *Histoire* (12.23.81) and begins thus: "Sire, you have more need of advice than of consolation. What you will do in the next hour will mark, for good or ill, the rest of your life, and will make you king, or nothing."

CHAPTER 6

1. D'Aubigné's account leaves a large gap between the death of Henry III and the fighting around Lagny in the summer of 1590. He had taken Cardinal de Bourbon, the League's candidate for king but Navarre's prisoner, from his cell in Chinon to Maillezais, where he was held until October 1589. During the winter of 1589–1590, while the new king was campaigning with some success in Normandy, Maine, Anjou, and Orleannais, d'Aubigné fought in some minor action in the south. Garnier (*Agrippa d'Aubigné*, 2:48–50) believed that he was

again with the king for the battle of Ivry (March 14, 1590), where Henry uttered his famous battle speech: "Companions! God is with us! There stand His enemies and ours. Here is your king. *A eux*! If your banners fall, rally to my white plume. You will find it on the road to victory and to honor" (*Histoire*, 13.6.189).

This victory was followed by the siege of Paris in the summer of 1590. The capital would have capitulated but for the intervention of a Spanish army from the Netherlands under the prince of Parma. Henry had to gather his scattered forces and march against this threat, thus ending the siege. Parma avoided a pitched battle and seemed content with the relief of Paris and a few minor victories, like the one at Lagny. Frustrated by the lengthening and fruitless campaign, Henry's gentlemen officers began to slip away.

2. After skirmishing with Parma's army d'Aubigné returned to Poitou (October 1590), where he fought a number of minor actions against local League forces.

3. These actions followed the siege of Rouen in the fall and winter of 1591–1592, when Henry's army included contingents of Englishmen. The incident involving Edmont occurred at Folleville on January 29, 1592, when the Englishman, seeing d'Aubigné in danger, jumped at the chance to "taster ceste meslee." Arumbure was the same gentleman whom d'Aubigné's men wounded in the confusion of an attack on Niort (*Histoire*, 13.15.257, 259–261).

4. In another action in the course of the siege of Rouen the king led a charge by spurring his horse directly over a steep gully. D'Aubigné in the *Histoire* records that he and the English officer did not dare follow but took a longer and safer route to join the action. "Here I name myself, to give glory to my master at the expense of one of the most valiant men in the world, and my own" (*Histoire*, 13.14.255).

5. This was at the siege of Dreux in June 1593. Much had hap-

pened since the siege of Rouen to show that Henry could never wear the crown of France as long as he remained a heretic. At the same time his popularity and the legitimacy of his claim excluded any possible rival. The necessity of his conversion had become evident, and by May of 1593 he formally announced his intention of making it. D'Aubigné, who had been skirmishing in his home region during the preceding winter, went to Dreux to try to dissuade Henry in a speech quoted in the *Histoire* (13.24.337–340).

6. After his mission to Dreux d'Aubigné returned to Poitou for the siege of Poitiers (June–July 1593) held for the League by Brissac.

7. The siege of La Fère, an episode in the war with Spain that broke out in 1595, took place from November of that year until May 1596. D'Aubigné's wife would thus have died in late 1595. His narrative has skipped over Henry IV's carefully managed conversion to Catholicism, which made possible his coronation at Chartres in February 1594.

8. D'Aubigné may refer here to a meeting of ministers and gentlemen at Saint-Maixent in April 1593, where he and a few others mapped out a plan of action to assure Protestant rights in the prospect of Henry's conversion.

9. Gabrielle d'Estrées, duchess of Beaufort, was Henry's current mistress.

10. His lip had been cut by Jean Chastel in an attempted assassination on December 27, 1594.

11. Henry's son by Gabrielle d'Estrées, born in 1594.

12. Because of his abjuration.

13. This was the meeting referred to above, note 8.

14. A permanent assembly met in the cities named from April 1, 1596, until February 11, 1598. Garnier (*Agrippa d'Aubigné*, 2:117–149) has given a succinct account of its actions to work out the terms of what would be the Edict of Nantes. Henry, now that he was king, wished to hold concessions to a minimum,

and he used his considerable powers with skill to erode the rugged resistance of his former allies. D'Aubigné distinguished himself as one of the *fermes*.

15. Canaye did not abjure (*se révolter* in d'Aubigné's words) until 1601, when he became ambassador to Venice.

16. "The goat of the desert," or scapegoat. D'Aubigné must have taken pride in the epithet because he used its initials LBDD to identify himself as author of *Les Tragiques* in the first edition.

17. D'Aubigné here has reverted to events that took place several years before. See chapter 5, note 39, and note 1 above.

18. See above chapter 4, note 15.

19. This was a theological debate held at Fontainebleau on May 4, 1600, in which Du Plessis was bested by his opponent, Jacques Davy du Perron, bishop of Evreux. The latter, one of the outstanding personalities of the time, had been raised a Protestant but converted to Catholicism at the court of Henry III. He was renowned for his learning and oratory, his charm, his connections. He preached the memorial service for Ronsard at Coqueret, negotiated Henry IV's papal absolution, introduced Malherbe to the court. D'Aubigné admired him but could not abide his success as the *convertisseur* who led prominent Huguenots into the Catholic church.

20. D'Aubigné provided more information about this debate in a letter published in the *Oeuvres complètes*, 1:373–382, but the treatise has disappeared.

21. The reference is to his opposition to Turenne, now the dúke of Bouillon, who had proposed that the Huguenot party support a plot hatched by the duke of Savoy. Among persons enticed into the affair was Biron's son, who paid with his head in 1602.

22. La Trémouille, one of the stalwarts in the Huguenot cause, died on October 25, 1604.

23. Garnier (*Agrippa d'Aubigné*, 2:317–318) dramatized this return

to the court at the end of 1604 or early 1605 by setting it in the context of d'Aubigné's depression at the loss of La Trémouille and the steady decline of the party. But he also pointed out a discrepancy with the letters received from Bouillon, since the latter, compromised by young Biron in the conspiracy of the duke of Savoy, was at the time in exile in Heidelberg.

24. Pierre Jeannin was president of the Parlement of Dijon and served as chief adviser for the League. He entered the service of Henry IV after the abjuration.

25. Garnier (*Agrippa d'Aubigné*, 2:321–322) described and analyzed the sparring between d'Aubigné and Sully at this assembly, which met in 1605. The latter, Maximilien de Béthune, baron of Rosny, not yet duke of Sully, was himself a Huguenot and a veteran of the wars, but he was above all the king's man. He served Henry IV well as minister of finance and made possible the internal improvements and economic recovery that marked Henry's reign. On this occasion the king had sent him to observe the assembly and see that it complied with pre-scribed procedures.

26. This refers to one of the two major issues confronting the assembly. The Edict of Nantes had provided for eight security places for eight years, a term that was about to expire. Sully had in his pocket a royal authorization for a four-year exten-sion, which he used as leverage to force compliance on the second issue, which concerned the manner of electing deputies-general, the official representatives of the church to the king. The edict called for the assembly to name a slate of six candidates from which the king would select two. Now the assembly wished to name the deputies directly.

27. At the heart of the matter was a quarrel between Blaccons, governor of Orange, and Lesdiguières, governor of Dauphiné.

28. The manuscript reads three months, but this must be a copy-ist's error for three years, since the events in question took place in 1607.

29. This council met in 451.

30. D'Aubigné described this episode in detail in a letter (*Oeuvres complètes*, 1:386–389).

31. She was the widow of François de Coligny, the admiral's son.

32. The project of sending d'Aubigné to Germany might have been discussed at any time between 1608 and his last visit to Henry in December 1609. The king was evidently making diplomatic moves preparatory to challenging the Habsbourg hegemony, perhaps as part of the "Great Design" which, as described by d'Aubigné in an appendix to the *Histoire* printed in vol. 9, pp. 465–467, was a plan to weaken Spain by freeing Italy and Flanders from her control, and by wresting the imperial crown from the Habsburgs.

33. On May 14, 1510, Henry was stabbed in the heart by Jacques Clément, the blow that d'Aubigné had prophesied.

CHAPTER 7

1. The queen was Marie de Médicis, whom Henry married in 1600 after the annulment of his marriage to Marguerite. In 1601 she gave birth to the future Louis XIII. Immediately after Henry's death she was declared queen regent by the Parlement of Paris and by the magnates of the kingdom.

2. Soon after the queen was made regent the deputy-general of the Huguenot party requested of her, and was accorded, a confirmation of rights under the terms of the Edict of Nantes. In return, a delegation went to Paris to make a formal submission to her. D'Aubigné, as will be seen, took the opportunity to show that his people were loyal but not subservient.

3. According to a letter discovered by Jean Plattard and published in the *Revue du seizième siècle* (10, [1924]:71–90), d'Aubigné requested this meeting so he might advise the queen about her policies.

4. This was an important assembly, not for what it accomplished but for what it revealed. The delegates, including d'Aubigné,

tried to test the queen regent by demanding additional concessions from her government. These included the right to name their own governors, to maintain additional strongholds, and to elect their deputies-general directly. They also proposed the creation of a new assembly, *l'assemblée du cercle*, as a regional organization to bridge the gap between the standing provincial assemblies and the cumbersome general assembly. The queen and her advisers rejected these demands and insisted on strict compliance with the Edict of Nantes. To break the ensuing deadlock the queen finally warned that she would deal only with those delegates who were willing to cooperate. Her threat was effective and it showed how a wedge could be driven between the zealots, or *fermes*, and the moderates, or *prudents*, for the assembly yielded, and the Huguenot party closed the session fatally weakened. The *fermes* remained strong enough, however, to maintain a stubborn tension with the government and to mount an occasional revolt until their political ambitions were finally crushed by Richelieu. D'Aubigné was inspired by the politics of the assembly to write his tract *Le Caducée ou l'ange de la paix* (*Oeuvres complètes*, 2:73–109).

5. When he was the viscount of Turenne, Bouillon had been one of Henry's strongest lieutenants and d'Aubigné's good friend. But his flirtation with Biron's conspiracy, his exile, and his slow return to grace had evidently tempered his Huguenot ardor.

6. Henry de Rohan (1579–1638) was a hothead who provoked the court repeatedly and led several insurrections during the regency and the early reign of Louis XIII. On this occasion he dismissed the royal lieutenant at Saint-Jean-d'Angély and installed his own man. Then, in defiance of the government, he called a local assembly at La Rochelle to seek justification of his action. Du Plessis was able to intervene and calm the situation.

7. D'Aubigné's appointment as governor of Maillezais included a stipend of 7,000 francs to pay the garrison. He was offered a

5,000-franc increment at Saumur, which he viewed as a bribe. When he rejected it the original stipend was suspended. He went to the Sèvre to levy tolls on river traffic.

8. "The mouse with one hole." D'Aubigné supported Rohan in his provocations and seemed quite willing to join in any eventual conflict. Le Dognon was an island in the marshes of the lower Sèvre, a few miles south of Maillezais. D'Aubigné would fortify it as an outpost to protect his main base.

9. The court under the regency soon split into quarreling factions. Henry II de Bourbon, third prince of Condé, proclaimed himself the leader of some of the disaffected elements and in a manifesto of February 1614 called for an insurrection. But he aroused little support and a reconciliation was effected in May.

10. Condé's second insurrection, launched with his manifesto of August 9, 1615, was more serious than the first. The ascendancy at court of ultramontane Catholics and the proposed Spanish marriages (Louis XIII to Anne of Austria; his sister Elizabeth to the son of Philip III) had created concern. The Huguenots were especially disturbed by these signs of rapprochement with Spain and of an increase in papal influence at court. Condé thus found serious support for his movement in Languedoc, Guyenne, and Poitou, where Bouillon, Rohan, and d'Aubigné rallied to his cause. The war that followed aroused little popular support, however, and since the marriages did take place there was little reason to prolong it. A peace was negotiated in early 1616.

11. Josué de Caumont of Ade had married Marie d'Aubigné in 1613 and thus was d'Aubigné's son-in-law.

12. Benjamin de Rohan, lord of Soubise, was Henry de Rohan's brother.

13. The quip was prophetic. Soon after returning to Paris Condé was imprisoned and held until 1620. For more on d'Aubigné's feelings about Condé, see his letter to Rohan (*Oeuvres complètes*, 1:348).

14. D'Aubigné had printed *Les Tragiques* in 1616 on his own press at Maillé. Jean-Louis de Nogaret of La Valette, duke of Epernon, had been a *mignon* of Henry III, who named him commander of infantry. He might well have inspired one of the satirical portraits of Henry III's courtiers in *Princes*. In 1616 he was made governor of Aunis and Saintonge.

15. The arrest of Condé, September 1616, alarmed the council of La Rochelle, so as a precaution to protect the city's interests Rochefort was occupied. Epernon, the new governor of Aunis-Saintonge, took this as a personal challenge, gathered an army, and made threatening moves against the city, which in turn took measures to defend itself. The government, faced by a threatened uprising of the nobility in support of the imprisoned Condé, was not about to let another war begin, so negotiations were started to settle the dispute.

16. The story of the Capuchin and his effect on the cardinal's nephew is told in *Les Tragiques: Feux*, vv. 1205–1222.

17. The Congregation for the Propagation of the Faith, created to supervise foreign missions, was not instituted until January 6, 1622, when d'Aubigné was settled in Geneva. This passage, written much later, shows perhaps some confusion in d'Aubigné's mind between the Congregation and an earlier intelligence operation.

18. The title means "Commentary on the Grisons." In his *Traité sur les guerres civiles*, d'Aubigné elaborated on the interrogation of Baronius's nephew, adding that he himself was shown "an excellent account of [our] strongholds, of the governors who had been suborned, and of those yet to be won; and little has since happened in fact that has not conformed to what was there in prospect" (*Oeuvres complètes*, 2:14).

19. La Rochelle capitulated October 8, 1628, so d'Aubigné clearly wrote this portion of the text after that date. Further information about the deaf-mute is given in the third of his "Lettres touchant quelques poincts de diverses sciences," *D'Aubigné: Oeuvres*, Pléiade edition, pp. 835–839.

20. Assemblies had convened at La Rochelle in November 1616 and again in April 1617 to deal with the threatening moves of Epernon. D'Aubigné made known to the delegates his desire to sell his properties at Maillezais and Le Dognon, probably for financial reasons, since their maintenance was becoming a burden to him. Epernon would have been eager to obtain them.

21. Villeroy was a secretary of state.

22. D'Aubigné's anger masks an unfortunate dilemma: while the two strongholds represented his personal fortune, the authorities in La Rochelle believed that the security of the city would be better assured if they were demolished.

23. Bertrand de Vignoles had been a page at the court of Navarre when d'Aubigné was squire. He was in the region to settle the quarrel between Epernon and La Rochelle.

24. The sale of the forts to Rohan was concluded April 29, 1619. D'Aubigné remained as Rohan's lieutenant at Maillezais, but pressure from the king's council forced him to leave and to settle at Saint-Jean-d'Angély before the end of the year.

    The circumstances surrounding the publication of the *Histoire universelle* are described by Garnier (*Agrippa d'Aubigné*, 3:71–85). D'Aubigné had printed the first two tomes, or volumes, on his own press between 1616 and 1618, but withheld them in the hope of obtaining a royal privilege for their publication. When this was not forthcoming he released them late in 1619. They were promptly condemned in Paris (January 2, 1620). In the meantime he set about printing the third tome, which was released in 1620.

CHAPTER 8

1. This "little war" followed Marie de Médicis's second attempt to incite an uprising against Louis XIII's council. The first one followed her banishment to Blois after the murder of her favorite, Concino Concini. On that occasion only Epernon an-

swered her call, and she had no choice but to settle with her son (April 30, 1619). In 1620 she called for a second rebellion, this time receiving a more serious response, which included the support of the Huguenot captains Rohan and Soubise.

2. The rebels' army had been put to flight at Ponts-de-Cé on August 7, 1620, and the uprising collapsed.

3. The Peace of Angers, signed August 10, 1620.

4. Louis XIII pursued his success at Ponts-de-Cé by advancing deep into the southwest, where he reestablished Catholicism in Béarn and generally imposed his authority in the Kingdom of Navarre. This would lead to the definitive integration of that state into France.

5. This man might have been a relative or descendant of the Anières who was d'Aubigné's first military commander.

6. D'Aubigné's illegitimate son Nathan, who had accompanied him into exile, married Pelissari's daughter in 1622; Sarrasin was the grandson of the man in whose house d'Aubigné lived when he was a student in Geneva.

7. This war council was created in September 1621 following events in France and elsewhere (Louis XIII's march into Béarn, the suppression of a revolt in Bohemia, etc.) that seemed to threaten the Protestant cause in Europe. D'Aubigné could not have known that he and the Genevans were responding to the first actions of the Thirty Years' War.

8. Saint-Victor was a suburb on the southeast side of the old city; Saint-Jean was to the north. D'Aubigné writes more about these projects later.

9. The assembly was called in La Rochelle in the autumn of 1620 following Louis XIII's march into the southwest. The delegates made demands upon the king and, when these were rejected, threatened an uprising.

10. The confusion in this sentence may be cleared up by reference to the composition of d'Aubigné's war council, four members of which came from the the Petty Council of Geneva, or the Twenty-Five, and three from the Council of Sixty. Two from

the first group were evidently appointed to help d'Aubigné draft his reply to the assembly at La Rochelle. To ensure their discretion he called upon their two colleagues of the war council for support.

11. Count Ernst von Mansfeld, a war leader in the service of the Protestant Union, which had formed to support the rebels of Prague, was defeated by the imperial forces of Ferdinand II at the battle of the White Mountain, November 1620. He managed to extricate a substantial portion of his army, however, and was available for new employment. D'Aubigné will try to enlist him and other German leaders to assist the French Huguenots.

12. Mansfeld invaded France to relieve military pressure on the Huguenots in Languedoc, but he was diverted by the duke of Nevers, governor of Champagne. Subsequently, with English and Dutch reinforcements, and in time French subsidies, he campaigned against imperial and Spanish armies in western Germany until he was finally beaten by Wallenstein in 1626. Despite his assurance d'Aubigné did not bring his supplement to the *Histoire universelle* up to these events.

13. D'Aubigné's account of his experiences in Berne may be clarified by reference to letters printed in the first volume of the *Oeuvres complètes* (pp. 137–139; 145–148; 204–205; 214–217; 217–220). He made two trips there, the first in November 1621, the second for three months in the spring of 1622. There was anxiety in the city because of the invasion of the Palatinate to the north by imperial troops. Still, there was opposition to fortifying the city because of the cost, the fear of drawing the hostile attention of the emperor, its location in the middle of its canton, etc. Opponents even sought the opinion of Bouillon, and he supported their objections. But d'Aubigné countered these arguments and evidently was instrumental in persuading the Bernese to assume the costs and risks of preparing for war. It was an effort, he wrote, to "awaken this sleeping bear" (*Oeuvres complètes*, 1:214).

14. Sieur de La Fosse was the title given to d'Aubigné's son Nathan.

15. The Venetian Republic, fearing war with Spain, proposed to d'Aubigné that he recruit Huguenot soldiers for their army. He jumped at the opportunity and was busily studying the geography of the mountains for secure routes (*Oeuvres complètes*, 1:292) when Venice and Savoy unexpectedly entered into a formal alliance with France (Treaty of Paris, February 7, 1623), which effectively ended the project.

16. A passage from this letter is quoted by Garnier (*Agrippa d'Aubigné*, 3:140). In it Louis expresses his displeasure at the protection given by Geneva to "certain of our subjects who have thrown off the yoke of the obedience and respect which they owe us."

17. The house was located near Jussy, about 10 km. east of Geneva.

18. The stone would have been used for the fortification of Maillezais, which d'Aubigné began in 1613.

19. The bride was Renée Burlamachi, born in Montargis in 1568 and a widow since 1621.

20. D'Aubigné's sentence was executed in effigy, *en tableau*, in Paris on the Place de Grève.

21. The owner was Michel Rozet, whose hostility would continue to trouble d'Aubigné.

22. D'Aubigné was authorized to reprint his history in Geneva in 1622, but permission was later withdrawn under the fear, propagated by his enemies, that publication would offend the French court. The book was nevertheless printed, but with place of publication given as Amsterdam.

23. George Frederick, margrave of Baden-Durlach, had been exiled by the emperor and had settled in Geneva. It was alleged that he and d'Aubigné were plotting to gather an army and attack Constance.

24. This Rozet was a son of the man whose property had been confiscated for the construction of the wall that d'Aubigné had designed. He and Sarrasin went to Paris in 1627 to claim pay-

ment of subsidies owed to Geneva. In their report to the Petty Council on their meeting with the secretary they included this observation: "We were surprised when, in a cool and low voice, [Herbaud] reproached us, saying: 'You gentlemen profess to support the interests of the king, and yet you harbor in your city his enemies, like d'Aubigné, who has written and continues to write, as well as to act, against the service of the king. Indeed you pay him honor. But did not his own son, now in Bordeaux, go to England to communicate with the enemies of the king after having visited his father in your city?'" (quoted by Garnier, *Agrippa d'Aubigné*, 3:169–170). To allay this criticism it was asserted in response that he was not a citizen and that since his marriage he had been living quietly at Le Crest. But to validate this defense d'Aubigné was restricted to his estate for three months.

The reference to the son is accurate, as the text will show. And the background that d'Aubigné described is also accurate: the Huguenots had lost their strongholds; La Rochelle was under siege; and in Germany, Catholic imperial forces seemed triumphant on all fronts.

25. Henry de Nogaret of Epernon, duke of Candale, a Protestant, was a son of the duke of Epernon.

26. Cardinal Richelieu joined the king's council in April 1624 and immediately set about his plan to challenge Habsburg hegemony in Europe. He first sent French forces into Valtellina to expel papal troops that occupied that territory for Spain. Soon after, another army, commanded by Lesdiguières, still governor of Dauphiné and (since his conversion in 1622) the *connétable*, was ordered to cross the Alps and attack Genoa, Spain's ally. D'Aubigné was consulted on the disposition of the Swiss cantons relative to these campaigns. This led to further consultations for another project, a diversionary attack on Franche-Comté, at that time a Spanish province vital for communications and troop movements between Italy and the Spanish Netherlands.

27. When the campaign against Genoa encountered difficulties it was reinforced with troops gathered for the invasion of Franche-Comté.

28. Carlisle was the English ambassador to Savoy; his brother was Thomas Rowe. They were in Geneva in July 1628.

29. Constant probably attended the Protestant college that flourished at the time in Sedan, a city acquired by Turenne-Bouillon at his marriage and situated along an uncertain Franco-imperial border.

30. Constant married Anne Marchant, a widow, in 1608. In February 1619 he surprised her with a lover and killed them both, a crime of passion for which he was later pardoned.

31. Father Arnoux, a Jesuit and friend of Du Perron, was Louis XIII's confessor. D'Aubigné conceded in a letter (*Oeuvres complètes*, 1:342) that Constant's conversion to Catholicism was not certain. What he had clearly become was a *libertin*, or free-thinker, in the father's view an even more distasteful choice.

32. The attempt on Le Dognon would have occurred between May 1619, when d'Aubigné sold the place, and the following December, when he had to leave it. Constant escaped capture at that time but was later arrested and held until July 1620, when he was freed on the intervention of the court.

33. Constant arrived in Geneva, full of contrition, early in 1624. The ministers imposed as a penance that he make public confession of his sins in the places where he had given scandal. He complied, and for a time d'Aubigné felt that he had reformed, for he was able to write to Rohan's wife, who also had a son who went astray: "I urge you to take the same resolve as I [did in threatening a complete break] and which, thank God, has succeeded; for the lost has been found and the dead resurrected" (*Oeuvres complètes*, 1:399).

34. This was in fact the king of Denmark, Christian IV, who supported the Protestant cause in Germany before the intervention of Gustavus Adolphus.

35. Constant's trip to England followed a visit to his father in

February 1627, a time when England and France still seemed to be testing a kind of rapprochement for mutual support against Spain and when traditional antagonisms were softened by the marriage of Louis XIII's sister, Henrietta Marie, to Charles I. But French policy suddenly veered to favor Spain, first with the Peace of Monzon in 1626, then the Treaty of Madrid in November 1627. The king of England's minister, George Villiers, duke of Buckingham, was embarrassed by the turn of events. To restore his credit he made overtures to potential allies in France, particularly to the Huguenots of La Rochelle, whose revolt he encouraged. In July 1627 he supported their rebellion with a fleet and 8,000–10,000 soldiers, who landed on the island of Ré. But by November his forces had to withdraw and the royal siege of La Rochelle was under way.

36. On his return to France after this last visit to his father, Constant was arrested; he was held a prisoner of state until the death of Richelieu in 1642.

37. The capitulation of La Rochelle in October 1628 marked the end of the political power of the Huguenots and freed Richelieu to pursue the main objective of Louis XIII's reign, the destruction of Habsburg hegemony in Europe. His next move was to support the claim of Charles of Gonzaga to the Duchy of Mantua against a Spanish claimant. The fear in Geneva was that the duke of Savoy would exploit the situation and attack her territory.

38. D'Aubigné died of his ailments on May 9, 1630, his last days disturbed by a storm of indignation aroused by the publication of the racy fourth book of his *Aventures du baron de Faeneste*. He was nevertheless buried with honor in the cloister of the former cathedral of Saint Peter.

History was to bestow an ironic honor on this champion of the Huguenot cause: his son Constant, imprisoned for his mysterious and probably treasonous adventures in England, seduced and later married the sixteen-year-old daughter of the governor of his first prison, the Château-Trompette in Bordeaux. Incarceration did not prevent him from fathering three more children by her. One of them, Françoise, born in 1635 in Niort, after a life of vicissitude and poverty, which included marriage to the novelist Paul Scarron, became the mistress and then, as Madame de Maintenon, the wife of Louis XIV, the king of France who in 1685 revoked the Edict of Nantes.

Index

Achon, Chevalier de, 7, 9, 131 n.7
Ade, Josué de Caumont, Sieur d',
    94, 117, 165 n.11
Agen, 38, 40–41
Albanians, 48–49, 146 n.7
Alençon, 28
Alençon, Francis, Duke of, 22, 70,
    138 n.11, 140 nn. 13, 16, 143 n.1,
    146 nn. 9, 148 nn. 1, 3
Amboise, 6, 10; Conspiracy or Tu-
    mult of, 20, 123, 130 n.4, 137 n.7;
    Edict of (1563), 132 n.11
Angers, 60; Peace of, 167 n.3
Angoulême, 12, 13
Anières, 13, 16, 17, 104, 167 n.5
Anjou, Duke of, 138 n.11. *See also*
    Henry III
Anne of Austria, 164 n.10
Antoine de Bourbon, xiv, 123
Arambure, Jean d', 36, 71, 74,
    156 n.34, 158 n.3
Archiac, 16, 54, 129 n.2
Arza, Louis d', 133 n.16

Aubigné, Constant d', x, 3, 116 ff.,
    171 nn. 29–32, 172 nn. 33, 35–36,
    173 n.38
Aubigné, Françoise d', 173 n.38
Aubigné, Jean d', 5, 8 ff., 20, 22, 54,
    129 n.2, 130 n.4
Aubigné, Nathan d', 110, 129 n.1,
    167 n.6, 169 n.14
Aubin d'Abeville, 10, 12, 129 n.2,
    132 n.13

Baronius, Gaspard, 97
Barricades, Day of (12 May, 1588),
    154 n.27, 155 n.30
Bartholomew, Saint, 19, 123, 126,
    137 n.5
Basel, 109 ff.
Bastille, 88, 95
Bayonne, 38
Beauce, 20
Beaugency, 19
Beaulieu, Peace of (1576), 142 n.25
Beauvoir-sur-Mer, 68

Bellarmine, Robert, 66, 152 n.20

Belle Isle, 79

Bergerac, Peace of (1577), 40, 144 n.11

Berne, 108–9, 168 n.13

Béroalde, Mathieu, 6 ff., 11, 130 n.5

Bèze, Théodore de, 11, 131 n.6, 132 n.14

Biron, Armand de Gontaut, Baron of, 47, 64, 71, 146 n.6, 152 n.18, 161 n.21, 163 n.5

Blaye, 46–47, 145 n.5

Blois, 18, 32, 156 n.30, 33

Bordeaux, 39

Bougouin, René de Vivonne, Lord of, 53 ff.

Bouillon. *See* Turenne

Boulogne, Edict of (1573), 138 n.11

Bourbon, Charles de, Cardinal, 78, 149 n.8, 157 n.38; House of, vii, xiv, 123–24

Bourges, 104

Briançon, 98

Brouage, 60, 63, 150 n.11

Buckingham, Georges Villiers, Duke of, 118, 172 n.35

Burlamachi, Renée, 112, 169 n.19

Bussy d'Amboise, Louis de Clermont, Lord of, 24 ff., 141 n.19, 147 n.14

Cadillac, 51, 146 n.9, 147 n.12

Calais, 131 n.6

Campion, Edmund, 65, 152 n.20

Canaye, Philippe, 77–78, 160 n.15

Candale, Henri de Nogaret, Duke of, 115, 171 n.25

Candalle, François de, Bishop of Aire, 51–52, 147 n.12

Carlisle, Count of, 115, 119, 171 n.28

Carnavalet, Françoise de, 26, 141 n.20

Casimir. *See* John Casimir

Castel-Jaloux, 36 ff., 45, 47

Castelnau-de-Mesme, 39–40

Catherine de Bourbon, 30, 58, 142 n.29

Catherine de Médicis, xii–xiv, 22, 32, 52, 121, 130 n.6, 132 n.11, 133 n.18, 134 nn. 19, 22, 136 nn. 3, 4, 137 nn. 5, 7, 145 n.2, 147 n.13, 152 n.22

Charles V, Emperor, 123 ff.

Charles IX, King of France, xiii, 22, 121, 130 n.6, 136 n.3, 138 n.11, 140 n.15, 147 n.15

Chastel, Jean, 160 n.10

Châteauneuf, 28

Châteauroux, 103

Châtellerault, 77, 84, 134 n.22

Chinon, 55, 78, 158 n.1

Clément, Jacques, 157 n.38, 162 n.33

Cognac, 16

Coligny, Gaspard de, xiv, 12, 122–23, 133 nn. 18, 19, 134 n.22, 136 n.3, 137 n.5

Colloquy of Passy, 131 n.6

Condé, Henri I de Bourbon, Prince of (1552–1588), xiv, 15, 53, 59–60, 123, 140 n.16, 141 n.24, 142 n.25, 143 n.1, 146 n.9, 150 n.11, 151 n.13

Condé, Henri II de Bourbon (1588–1646), 93 ff., 116, 123–24, 164 nn. 9–10, 165 nn. 13, 15

Condé, Louis I de Bourbon (1530–1569), xiv, 6, 10, 130 nn. 4, 6, 133 nn. 18, 19, 134 n.22, 135 n.25

Constable, the. *See* Montmorency, Anne de

Constans, Jacques de, 36, 46, 52, 58

Cottin, Jean, 5, 130 n.3

Courance, 7

Coutras, 15; battle of, 153 nn. 25–27

Damville, Henri de Montmorency, Count of, 24, 33, 122, 139 n.11, 143 nn. 3, 5

Démocarès, 7, 131 n.7

Dreux, 9, 131 n.6, 132 n.10, 159 nn. 5, 6

Du Perron, Jacques Davy, 80–81, 85 ff., 160 n.19, 171 n.31

Du Plessis-Mornay, Philippe, 68, 78, 80, 155 n.29, 160 n.19, 164 n.6

Duras, Madame de, 52, 147 n.14

Elizabeth I, xv

Enfants perdus, 16, 72, 135 n.26

England, xv, 115, 118–19, 136 n.3, 151 n.11, 172 n.35

Entragues, François de Balzac, 53, 147 n.15

Epernon, Jean-Louis de Nogaret, Duke of, 95, 100–101, 115, 148 n.3, 165 nn. 14, 15, 166 nn. 20, 23, 167 n.1, 171 n.25

Estang, Catherine de l', 5

Fervacques, Guillame de Haute-mer, Lord of, 22 ff., 54, 140 n.13

Fleix, Peace of (1580), 145 n.2, 146 n.9

France, Renée de, Duchess of Ferrara, 8, 132 n.8

Franche-Comté, xi, 115, 171 nn. 26, 27

Francis II, xiii, 121 ff., 130 nn. 4, 6

Gabrielle d'Estrées, 160 n.9

Gascony, 33, 47

Geneva, ix, 11, Chapter 8 passim

Germany, 23, 42, 88, 114, 119, 162 n.32, 170 n.24

Graffenried, Antoine, 108–9

Guicciardini, Francesco, 86

Guiche, Diane d'Andouins, Countess of, 57–58, 68, 149 n.4

Guise, Francis I, Duke of (1519–1563), 121–22, 130 nn. 4, 6; Henri, 23 ff., 71, 122, 140 n.16, 149 n.8, 153 n.27, 155 n.30, 156 n.33

Guitres, 59, 149 n.8

Habsbourg, House of, xv, 162 n.32, 171 n.26

Hampton Court, Treaty of, 131 n.6

Henry II (1519–1559), xiii, 122

Henry III (1551–1589), xiii, 24, 73, 122–23, 138 n.11, 139 n.12, 141 n.19, 148 nn. 1, 3, 149 n.8, 152 n.22, 153 n.27, 156 n.33, 157 nn. 37, 38, 165 n.14

Henry IV (1553–1610), vii, viii, x, xiii–xv, 3, 22 ff., 27 ff., Chapters 3–6 passim, 99, 122, 123–24

January, Edict of (1562), 131 n.6, 132 n.11

Jarnac, 14, 48, 134 n.22

Jazeneuil, 14, 134 n.22

Jeannin, Pierre, 82, 100

John Casimir, 41, 44, 133 n.17, 142 n.25

Joinville, Treaty of (1584), 149 n.8

Joyeuse, Anne, Duke of, 24, 66, 152 n.22, 153 nn. 23–27

July, Edict of (1585), 150 n.8, 152 n.22

La Boulaye, Charles Eschallart, Lord of, 30, 42, 44–45, 48, 58, 142 n.28, 145 n.4

La Fosse, Sieur de. *See* d'Aubigné, Nathan d'

La Garnache, 171

La Magdaleine, François de, 36, 44–45, 144 n.8

La Mole, Boniface de, 139 n.11

La Noue, François de, 33–35, 39, 68, 84, 103, 143 n.4

La Renaudie, Jean du Barry, Sieur de, 130 n.20

La Rocheabeille, 14, 134 n.22

La Rochefoucauld, François, Count of, 47, 53, 62

La Rochelle, viii, xii, 20, 22, 51, 62 ff., 68, 79, 95, 99 ff., Chapter 8 passim, 137 n.6, 164 n.6, 165 n.15, 166 nn. 19–20, 166 n.23; Peace of (1573), 22, 138 n.11

La Trémouille, Claude, 81, 82–83, 161 n.22

Laval, Paul de Coligny, Count of, 60, 151 n.13

Laverdin, Jean de Beaumanoir, Marquis of, 29, 36, 38–39, 141 n.22, 144 n.6

League, the Holy, xiv, 82, 122, 142 n.25, 143 n.1, 149 n.8, 152 n.22, 153 n.27, 155 n.30

Le Crest, 111, 114, 170 n.24

Le Dognon, 93 ff., 116–17, 164 n.8, 166 n.20, 171 n.32

Lesdiguières, François de Bonne, Duke of, 84, 98, 115, 162 n.27, 171 n.26

Les Landes, 18, 128, 145 nn. 12, 13

Lezay, Suzanne de, 41, 53 ff., 56, 60, 75, 129 n.1, 145 n.12, 159 n.7

L'Hospital, Michel de, 20, 130 n.6, 137 n.7, 139 n.11

Libourne, 14, 49, 146 n.9

Limoges, 42, 44, 46

Limur, Anne de, 5, 129 n.2

Longjumeau, Peace of (1567), 133 n.18

Lorraine, House of, xiii, 121–22. *See also* Guise

Loudun, 77; Treaty of, 95

Louis XIII, 99, 103, 110, 118–19, 162 n.1, 164 n.6, 167 nn. 4, 7, 168 n.9

Louvre, 36, 137 n.5, 155 n.30

Lusignan, 94, 134 n.22

Lyons, 11, 133 n.16

Madame. *See* Catherine de Bourbon.

Maillé, 93, 165 n.14

Maillezais, 71–72, 78–79, 94–95, 101–2, 116–17, 157 nn. 35, 37, 158 n.1, 164 n.8, 166 nn. 20, 24, 169 n.18

Malherbe, François de, 160 n.19

Manifeste de Péronne, 150 n.8

Mansfeld, Ernst von, 107, 168 nn. 11, 12

Marguerite de Valois, 28, 44, 46, 52–53, 56, 59, 136 n.4, 141 n.19, 145 n.2, 146 n.9, 147 n.13, 148 nn. 1–2

Marie de Médicis, 90–91, 94, 102, 124, 162 n.1, 167 n.1

Matignon, Jacques de, 22, 153 n.27

Marot, Clément, 134 n.23

Mauzé, 95, 101

Mayenne, Charles de Lorraine, Duke of, 48, 122, 156 n.33

Mer, 20, 45, 135 n.1

Mercoeur, Philippe de Lorraine, Duke of, 59, 150 n.9

Milly, 7

Mirambeau, François de Pons, Lord of, 13, 33, 143 n.2

Miron, Robert, 110

Mons, 19

Monsieur. *See* Alençon, Duke of

Montaigne, Michel de, 154 n.27

Montaigu, 42, 46, 48, 145 n.4

Montargis, 8

Montauban, 45

Montcontour, 14

Montfort-L'Amaury, 27

Montgomery, Gabriel de Lorges, Count of, 22–23, 139 n.12, 140 nn. 13, 14, 16

Montmorency, Anne de, 9, 122, 131 n.6, 132 n.10; House of, xiii, 122

Morel, Jean, 5–6

Morvins, 96

Mursay, 99, 148 n.20

Nantes, 42, 145 n.4; Edict of (1598), 160 n.14, 161 n.26, 163 nn. 2, 4

Nemours, Treaty of (1585), 150 nn.8

Nérac, 36, 47, 145 n.2, 146 n.6

Netherlands, xi, xv, 136 n.3, 146 n.9, 158 n.1, 171 n.26

Nîmes, 94

Niort, 71, 117, 156 n.33, 173 n.38

Normandy, 22, 27, 139 n.13, 140 n.16, 158 n.1

Oléron, 60 ff.

Orange, 84, 162 n.27

Orléans, 6, 8 ff., 18–19, 21, 130 nn.6, 157 n.37

Paix de Monsieur. See Beaulieu, Peace of

Panigarola, Francesco, 65, 152 n.20

Paris, xii, 5–6, 19, 56, 72, 80, 85, 89–90, 98, 101–3, 112, 118–19, 154 n.27, 155 n.30, 157 n.38, 158 n.1, 162 n.1, 163 n.2, 167 n.24, 169 n.20

Pelissari, 105, 167 n.6

Peregim, 5

Périgord, 13

Philip II, xi, xv, 146 n.9, 150 n.8, 155 n.30

Picardy, 142 n.25

Poitiers, 56, 59, 75, 79, 90, 94, 134 n.22, 159 n.6

Poitou, xii, 41, 53, 58–60, 79, 89, 92, 94, 98, 103, 116, 118, 158 n.2, 159 n.6

Poland, xvi, 138 n.11, 139 n.12, 140 n.15

Pons, 5, 13–14, 134 nn. 21

Ponts-de-Cé, 103, 167 nn. 2, 4
Postel, Guillaume, 32, 138 n.10
Printemps, Le, vii, 19, 135 nn. 24, 2

Reîtres, xv, 154 n.27
Retz, Claude-Catherine de
    Clermont-Dampierre, Duchess
    and Maréchale of, 53, 54, 78,
    147 n.15
Richelieu, Armand-Jean du Plessis,
    vii, 163 n.4, 171 n.26, 172 nn. 36–
    37
Rohan, Henry, Duke of (1579–
    1638), 93, 101–3, 117–18, 164 n.6,
    166 n.24, 167 n.1, 172 n.33
Rohan, René (1541–1586), 60
Ronsard, Pierre de, 160 n.19
Rouen, 74, 158 n.3, 159 nn. 4–5
Royon, 17
Rozet, Michel, 114, 170 nn. 21, 24

Saintes, 13, 67
Saint-Gelais, castle of, 33, 41
Saint-Gelais, Louis de, 30, 33, 42,
    56, 59, 71, 142 n.28
Saint-Germain, Peace of (1570),
    133 n.20, 135 n.1
Saint-Jean [d'Angélys], 68, 71, 93,
    101, 102–3, 164 n.6, 166 n.24
Saint-Luc, Timoléon d'Espinay,
    Lord of, 63, 65
Saint-Maixent, 52, 77, 84, 103,
    147 n.13, 159 n.8
Saint-Maury, 5
Saintonge, xii, 12, 16, 76, 89, 95
Salviati, le Chevalier de, 22,
    137 nn.9

Salviati, Diane, 19, 21, 25, 128,
    135 n.2, 137 n.9
Salviati, Jean, 20, 135 n.2
Sancerre, 20, 137 n.6
Sarrasin, Jean, 105, 107, 114, 167 n.6,
    170 n.24
Saumur, 29, 77, 91 ff., 94, 115,
    164 n.7
Savignac, Jacques de Lambès, Lord
    of, 14–15, 18
Savoy, 105, 169 n.15, 173 n.37
Schomberg, Henri, Count of Nan-
    teuil, 119
Sedan, 107, 116, 171 n.29
Ségur, François de, 57 ff., 148 n.3
Soubise, Benjamin de Rohan,
    Lord of, 94, 165 n.12, 167 n.1
Spain, xi ff., 89, 98, 101, 136 n.3,
    155 n.30, 159 n.7, 162 n.32, 169 n.15,
    171 n.26, 172 n.35
Stances, Les, 136 n.2, 138 n.10
States General, 152 n.22, 154 n.27,
    156 nn. 30, 33
Sully, Maximilien de Bethune,
    Duke of, 84, 88–89, 94 ff.,
    161 nn. 25, 26
Surgères, 101

Taillebourg, 59, 67
Talcy, 19 ff., 127, 135 n.2
Talmont, 66
Thouars, 92
Tonnay-Charente, 95
Tours, 72
Tragiques, Les, vii, 38, 95, 126 ff.,
    137 n.5, 145 n.12, 160 n.16, 165 nn.
    14, 16

Turenne, Henri de la Tour, Viscount of, and Duke of Bouillon, 46, 68, 71, 77 ff., 81, 91, 93–94, 98, 107–8, 145 n.2, 161 nn. 21, 23, 163 n.5, 164 n.10, 169 n.13, 171 n.29

Union, Pact of (1588), 155 n.30

Vachonière, 33 ff.
Vatable, François, 6, 130 n.5

Vendôme, 77; Duke of, 76
Venice, 110, 169 n.15
Vignolles, Bertrand de, 100, 166 n.23
Villeneuve-Saint-Georges, 7
Villeroy, Nicolas de Neufville, Lord of, 90, 100, 166 n.21

William of Orange, 134 n.19, 146 n.9